LLEWELLYN'S

2020

Magical Almanac

Featuring

Elizabeth Barrette, Danielle Blackwood,
Blake Octavian Blair, Emily Carlin, Deborah Castellano,
Kerri Connor, Divina Cornick, Monica Crosson,
Raven Digitalis, Kate Freuler, Sasha Graham,
JD Hortwort, James Kambos, Lupa, Estha K. V. McNevin,
Daniel Moler, Thorn Mooney, Mickie Mueller,
Diana Rajchel, Silver RavenWolf, Melissa Tipton,
Charlynn Walls, Tess Whitehurst,
and Charlie Rainbow Wolf

Llewellyn's 2020
Magical Almanac

ISBN 978-0-7387-4945-7. Copyright © 2019 by Llewellyn Publications. All rights reserved. Printed in the United States. Llewellyn Publications is a registered trademark of Llewellyn Worldwide Ltd.

Editing and design by Lauryn Heineman
Cover illustration © Jennifer L. Meyer
Calendar pages design by Michael Fallon
Calendar pages illustrations © Fiona King

Interior Illustrations: © Elisabeth Alba: pages 2, 54, 57, 175, 178, 237, 240; © Kathleen Edwards: pages 26, 30, 35, 67, 70, 75, 207, 210, 262, 265; © Wen Hsu: pages 1, 29, 45, 48, 50, 55, 59, 68, 90, 93, 100, 107, 173, 181, 184, 208, 213, 224, 229, 232, 239, 266, 268; © Mickie Mueller: pages 38, 42, 96, 99, 215, 218, 221, 271, 275; © Silver RavenWolf: 103; © Eugene Smith: pages 10, 13, 61, 195, 198, 202, 245, 248; © Amber Zoellner: pages 16, 20, 22, 24, 189, 192, 251, 254, 258

All other art by Dover Publications and Llewellyn Art Department

Special thanks to Amber Wolfe for the use of daily color and incense correspondences. For more detailed information, please see *Personal Alchemy* by Amber Wolfe.

You can order Llewellyn annuals and books from New Worlds, Llewellyn's catalog. To request a free copy of the catalog, call 1-877-NEW-WRLD toll-free or visit www.llewellyn.com.

Astrological data compiled and programmed by Rique Pottenger. Based on the earlier work of Neil F. Michelsen.

Llewellyn Worldwide Ltd.
2143 Wooddale Drive
Woodbury, MN 55125

Table of Contents

Earth Magic

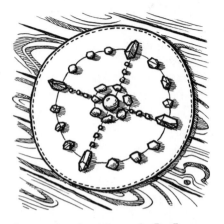

Crystal Grid Magic

Tess Whitehurst

When you start with a crystal-clear, rock-solid intention, creating a crystal grid is a powerful act of magic. Plus, it's fun to do, and fun always adds a generous dose of effectiveness to any work of magic. And let's not forget that upon completion of your grid, a beautiful mandala will have appeared in your space, shining with the unmistakable glow of enchantment and crafted out of the precious, sparkling minerals of the earth.

Crystal Grid Basics

Building a grid draws upon the structured strength of sacred geometry and the precise properties of powerful gems. There is a specific structure to the practice, but it's also a highly creative act that can be adapted according to your preference. So while these basic guidelines will assist you in constructing the crystal grids outlined in the next few pages, you can also use them to dream up your own designs that incorporate the crystals you happen to have available, as well as your own unique intentions and aesthetic taste.

First, state your intention. It's always most effective to do this in the present tense, as if already true. For example, if you choose to

create one of the grids below, you might state, "I am successful," "I am wealthy," or "I am in divine flow." In addition to composing the statement, add momentum to your intention by saying it aloud and writing it down somewhere, such as a journal or notebook.

Next, obtain or create a crystal grid cloth. This is a square of cloth, roughly twelve to fourteen inches on each side, depicting a sacred geometrical pattern. If you're not the crafty type, just search "crystal grid cloth" on Etsy and you'll find plenty of options. As an alternative to a cloth, you may use a geometrical pattern printed or drawn on paper, as long as it's big enough to comfortably fit your crystals. You'll want to select a pattern that possesses properties that are in alignment with your goal. The grids that follow incorporate three of the most popular designs for crystal grids: the flower of life (which promotes positive expansion), the seed of life (which holds the power of potent generation and endless multiplication), and Metatron's cube (which emanates precision, alignment with divine wisdom, and synchronization with the dance of the cosmos).

Then, assemble your crystals. For the grids that follow, you'll find lists of exactly what you'll need. Still, you may like to read over the following descriptions to get a working understanding of how it all works together. Of course, you'll also find this overview helpful when crafting your own grids.

To start, you'll need an anchor stone. This will be the most substantial piece in the grid: it's often a cluster, pyramid, or somewhat symmetrical standing crystal point. The anchor stone is the heart of the grid: it's important that its properties and the feeling it gives you are in strong alignment with what you're choosing to manifest.

You'll then need various stones to be positioned at strategic points on the mandala surrounding the anchor stone. You can think of these stones as carrying your intention outward from the anchor stone in concentric, vibrational waves, and radiating it into the world in perfect expression. (When creating your own design, follow your intuition about exactly what stones to choose and where to place them in the grid. You may also like to play around with crystal placement until it all seems to "click.")

Now, cleanse and empower your crystals. Cleansing removes any energetic debris and activates the metaphysical properties of the stones. If possible, bathe the stones in a clean body of flowing water, such as ocean waves or a mountain stream. (I like to use a metal strainer for this purpose when cleansing a bunch of crystals at a time.) If you don't have access to such a body of water, you can simply run them under cold water in a sink for two to three minutes or so. After cleansing the stones in water, allow them to bathe in bright sunlight for about five to ten minutes.

Finally, craft your grid. After spreading your cloth on a flat surface (and ironing it if necessary), begin with the anchor stone, which you will place at the exact center of the pattern.

From the anchor stone, work outward—in other words, begin with the circle of stones closest to the anchor stone, then move to the next circle outward, and so on. For any grids that you create in order to magnetize or summon a particular condition, place each stone in a clockwise manner. For grids created to banish, dissolve, or diminish, it will be more effective to place each stone in a counterclockwise manner.

Be aware that it's ideal to leave your grid in place for at least one moon cycle, or twenty-eight days. So choose your placement accordingly. While your grid will be effective no matter where you place it, if your space is big enough to provide more than one option, you may like to place your grid in the feng shui sector that is most in alignment with your grid's intention.

If you don't already know the feng shui areas of your home, here's a quick guideline to finding the areas ideal for the grids below. Keep in mind that if your floor plan is irregular (i.e., not shaped like a rectangle or square), or if you're crafting grids for alternate purposes, you'll need to do further research to discover where these are in your space. (See the resources section at the end of the article.)

While standing at the front door of your home, facing inward . . .

Your Helpful People and Travel area (perfect for the divine timing grid) will be on the far right of the side of your home closest to the front door, often the front of the house.

Your Fame and Reputation area (perfect for the success grid) will be in the center of the side of your home that is directly across from you, often the back of the house.

Your Wealth and Prosperity area (perfect for the abundance grid) will be in the farthest left corner of your home. This is just to the left of the Fame and Reputation area.

Success Grid

You will need:
Grid cloth depicting the flower of life
1 pyrite cluster (P)
6 tumbled hematites (H)
6 tumbled rubies (R)
6 tumbled rose quartzes (RQ)

This grid will supercharge your success and support you in spectacularly expressing your heart's desire.

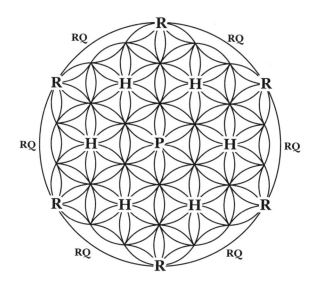

First, clearly state your success-related intention in the present tense. Place the pyrite (P) at the center to anchor your intention of establishing enjoyable, lasting success in your career or any endeavor. Next, place the hematites (H) as shown, in a clockwise manner, to infuse your success with calm, grounding, and divine orchestration. Again in a clockwise order, place the rubies (R) to symbolize the joy and vitality you feel when you share your passions with the world. Finish with the rose quartz (RQ) pieces to illustrate your success as an expression of devotion and loving interconnection.

Abundance Grid

You will need:

Grid cloth depicting the seed of life

1 clear quartz point that can stand upright (QP)

6 tumbled clear quartzes (Q)

6 tumbled carnelian (C)

6 tumbled aventurine (A)

6 citrine quartz points (CQ)

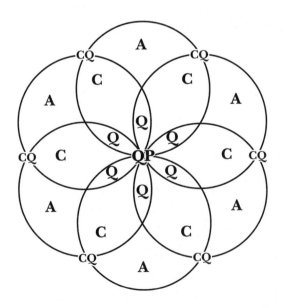

You can imagine this grid as a golden acorn that will give birth to endless oak forests of fortune.

After clearly stating your wealth-related intention in the present tense, place the quartz point (QP) at the center to tap into and energize an endless flow of wealth. To further energize and awaken this flow, place the six tumbled clear quartz (Q) around the anchor stone (moving clockwise) as shown. As mentioned for the Success Grid, place each successive circle of crystals in a clockwise order. To lend momentum to your confidence, as well as your natural ability to attract money easily and with joy, place the carnelians (C) as shown. Next place the aventurines (A) to open your heart to your own worthiness and to attune to the vibration of luck. Finally, arrange the citrine quartz points (CQ), pointing outward, to send all this magic out into the world and to emanate a powerfully magnetic energy that will irresistibly draw wealth and blessings of all varieties.

Divine Timing Grid

You will need:
Grid cloth depicting Metatron's cube
1 celestine cluster (C)
6 gray or light-colored tumbled agates (A)
6 small or medium clear quartz points (Q)
6 small tumbled sodalites (S)
6 small tumbled hematites (H)

This grid holds the energy of the vast order of the cosmos. Creating it welcomes a most auspicious and harmonious flow into your life experience.

Say or write, "I am in divine flow," or another divine timing–related intention (stated in the present tense). Then you're ready to place the celestine cluster (C) at the center to attune your grid to the consciousness of the cosmos and the frequency of the angelic realm. Moving in a clockwise direction (now and with each successive circle of stones), arrange the agates (A) as shown to align with

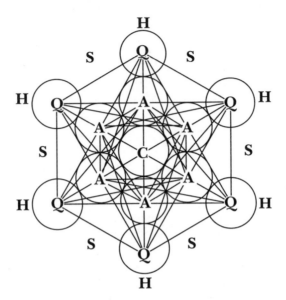

the perfect and precise orchestration of divine energy and wisdom. Next, create a clear channel of divine wisdom, guidance, and support by placing the quartz points (Q) as shown, making sure each is pointing outward. Place the sodalites (S) next to facilitate a sense of calm orderliness and confidence that everything is perfectly unfolding. Finally, position the hematites (H) to anchor the invisible harmony of the spheres in the visible realm of form.

Resources

Fogg, Kiera. *Crystal Gridwork: The Power of Crystals and Sacred Geometry to Heal, Protect, and Inspire*. Newburyport, MA: Weiser, 2018.

Lembo, Margaret Ann. *The Essential Guide to Crystals, Minerals, and Stones*. Woodbury, MN: Llewellyn, 2013.

Melody. *Love Is in the Earth: a Kaleidoscope of Crystals*. Wheat Ridge, CO: Earth Love Publishing House, 1995.

Seeding the Silence

Sasha Graham

I am writing to you from a late August afternoon, one of those days when the world wraps heat and warmth, sound and color all around you. The air is humid and thick. Sunlight is streaming through the kitchen windows. The light is heavy with the sound of cicadas and distant thunder from storms crashing through the mountains like waves. Everything is aglow with moisture and magic. Juicy tomatoes and forest-green zucchini that popped from the garden are now lounging on the counter, while cascading flowers tendril across outdoor stone walls and wooden posts. Spiders cast their invisible strands through the air and float across the grass, flickering under sunlit droplets though rustling poplar trees. The backyard feels like a hidden coral reef beneath the ocean.

Presence

It is easy to feel the energy, magic, and creative impulse pulsating around and through you on a day such as this. As easy as falling in love and feeling the world burst with enchantment and drip with glossy magic. The wise Witch knows that this power, this deliciousness, this energy of life, this magic, surrounds her and infuses her at all moments, even during her darkest days. Magic draws us forth, up and out of ourselves when we might otherwise drown. Awareness of magic between life's dramatic ebbs and flows, the depth of connecting to the energy powering all things, brings richness to the Witch's life. The deeper the Witch journeys, the greater her breadth of experience, the broader, vaster, and more expansive her pleasure. Dipping into this ecstasy, like cultivating sacred space, is enough in itself. The experience is greater than the material culmination of any spell, wish, or desire. The heart of magic hasn't to do with any result; rather, it propels the practitioner to the source of all experience.

There is a rich component of magic at your fingertips at all time. It surrounds you, envelops you, aids and abets you whether you know it or not. I want to teach you how to look for this. It is like a morning spiderweb, wet with dew. You have to be at the right angle to see it. You have to know it is there before you look for it, play with it, work with it, give it love, respect it, and cultivate it.

It is something that exists inside you and outside you. It is malleable like putty, clay, and it contains the secret to everything. Like divinity, it wants to be seen. It wants you to notice it. Once you recognize it, it will feel you feeling it. It will respond to your gaze and attention. It will wrap itself around you with a greater ecstasy than the most responsive lover.

This beautiful, eloquent, magical tool is silence.

Awakening

Silence may seem the most obvious thing in the world and no big deal, but stop and step back for a moment. Think about the obvious yet utterly miraculous fact that you opened your eyes and woke up this morning. Think about every great and seemingly obvious invention or assumption that was once inconceivable until we humans figured it out. We didn't always know the world was round, humanity wasn't born with a keen control over the element of fire, and we didn't figure out how to use three-point perspective to create sublime works of art until the Renaissance. So with an open mind, take my hand and let's walk toward the silence together. The door of possibility is waiting for you.

Silence is the sound of the universe. Silence is the essence of dark matter. Silence is the space of infinite possibility. Silence is the expansiveness in which the four elements of earth, air, fire, and water exist. Silence is the space between cards in a tarot spread. Silence is the space into which we enter to observe and understand another human being. Silence is a place in which the ego cannot exist because to truly embody silence there can be no ego. Silence is the space in which you make room for other people. Silence is where you become the acute and active observer of everything around you.

The Witch knows her true power lies in the possession of her inner world and her response to external stimuli. Silence, above all things, is the space between stimulus and reaction. Working with silence allows the Witch to choose her response to any and all things coming at or to her because she can stand inside of it. She becomes the active observer of her own consciousness and the world around her. The space in which she chooses her response is silence. Inside this silent space she expands, grows, and unfolds herself in the most authentic way possible. She no longer is a slave to her old patterning, emotions, and external circumstances.

To cast spells inside silent space you must become adept at cultivating, courting, and recognizing silence. Once you do, it is possible to place seeds of magical intention inside silence the same way you plant seeds in a garden. The universe continually unfolds. It becomes larger and more aware of itself in every moment. Silence is exactly the space where you want to place your desires, dreams, and heartfelt passions. Sort out and identify what is meaningful to you and place your intentions inside this stillness.

Cultivate Your Relationship with Silence

Your relationship with silence is one that is unique to you and only you. Your magical footprint, your sensibilities, empathies, and gifts are as unique as your body, your scent, and your kiss. Use the opportunity to commune with silence as a sacred compact between you and the universe (or whatever name/word you use for things divine in nature). Do not place any preconceived notions upon your experience. The relationship is personal and yours alone. It is for no one else's eyes or ears. No one feels a song as you do. No one experiences a poem like you do. It is the internal journey we all embark on. Our experience of the world happens inside us. It is between us and that which we came from. We are fortunate when we meet others who share inklings of what we feel and know, others who sense and recognize a similar tug of the soul. We feel immediate kinship with these people, those friends with whom a decade may have passed, yet ten years feels as swift as five minutes passing after finding each other again. Friends, lovers, children, writers, artists may awaken dormant desires inside of us yet; they may wedge open new possibilities, yet we still must venture into stillness alone.

To cultivate your relationship with silence, all you need to do is turn your attention toward it. The simplest thing you can do is listen for the silence inside your breath, between your inhale and exhale. Place your tongue gently behind your teeth to open up your throat palate. Seal your lips and slightly lower your chin while keeping your back straight. Close your eyes. Inhale, pause, and listen for silence. Exhale, pause, and listen for silence. Do this ten times. Do this every morning and evening. Increase by five counts very day.

Dedicate space inside your journal to writing about silence. Note your thoughts, feelings, and observations regarding silence. You can use any regular dedicated or ritualized time when you perform actions with focused attention, such as painting, crafting, running and so on, to examine the nature of silence. Do you practice yoga?

Find the silence inside your body. Do you dance or play music? Listen for the space between the notes. Are you an accountant? Look for the silence between numbers. It can be found everywhere once you look for it.

Cultivate your relationship with silence to transform moments of boredom into an adventure. Infinite doors to silence exist and wait for you to open them. No matter where you are at this very moment, turn your attention to the sounds surrounding you. Like a scientist, pull apart each sound. If you are sitting in an urban environment, decipher each and every sound. Note each sound: Do you hear a passing truck, a distant jackhammer, the hum of an air filter vent, the music from a passing car, the laughing sound of voices in the air? List everything you can hear. Then listen for the silence behind all those sounds. It is like the canvas behind the painting. Are you sitting in countryside? Can you hear crickets? The breeze rustling the trees? A distant fire whistle? Crows squawking to each other? Can you, after listing and listening for everything, hear the silence behind it all?

Cultivating your relationship with silence is a process that will take some time. Enjoy the journey and don't rush it. Think of it as a delicious new relationship. Savor the intricacies. As you explore silence in different places, begin thinking broadly about the seeds you would like to plant inside of it. Think of this as planting a garden. Just as you can plant tender greens in the spring garden, sunflowers in the summer garden, and scarlet beets in the fall garden, you can be actively cultivating the silence all year long and planting seeds inside the pockets of it.

Seeding the silence is also your opportunity to cast a spell with far-reaching implications. Chances are, the qualities you desire in your life are connected like roots in their underbellies. There will likely be common themes among different sectors of your life—love, career, family, creativity, and so on. You may desire a single specific object. You may wish to experience a deeper, more meaningful life. No matter what is important to you, dedicate part of your journal to the qualities you would like to attract and enhance in your life. Focus on the generalities rather than specifics. The universe will always be more creative and exciting in its delivery of your soul's desire than you could ever predetermine. It doesn't matter how wild and wonderful your imagination is. Remember this when casting your spells and weaving enchantments. Release control. Let the creative principle of the universe do its part. The universe gives us exactly what we need at all times. We don't always know what is best for us even when we want something more than anything else in the world. Trust in the wisdom of what is before you.

Seeding the Silence Ritual

Ingredients:
Candle
Dried lavender
Star tarot card
Dried flower petals or pieces of wood/dried bark
Pen

Once you have established a relationship with silence and have done the good work of thoughtfully considering exactly what you'd like to "plant," it is time to get to work. Plan a morning, afternoon, or evening when you can be alone and walk in nature. The time of day is up to your personal preference. You may go somewhere familiar or explore a new trail, park, or mountain. You may remain in your own backyard. Find a place that will feel expansive and beautiful to you.

Preceding your walk, open the four corners, smudge your sacred space with dried lavender, and light a white candle. (If possible, perform the entire ritual outside.) Place the Star tarot card beneath the candle and allow your consciousness to move inside the archetype. The Star card is the silence after the storm. It reflects crystalline, clear, inspired, open space and silence. Feel yourself becoming the figure on the card. Feel the flow between the waters and the land, the emotions and the material world. Imagine your energy connected to the ground beneath you and to the stars above. Venture further inside the card and yourself to feel the stellar energy illuminating you, making you. You are pure energy. Own it. Feel it. Luxuriate inside of it.

Remaining illuminated with luminosity, write your intentions, desires, or seeds fully and completely on dried flower petals or on the smooth back of dried wooden bark. Once they have been written, read each intention aloud. Close your sacred space and take your petals or wooden pieces outside with you. Embark on your walk into silence. Observe the silence as you have been doing in the previous weeks. Listen for it through all the sounds around you. You will instinctually know when you have found silence. You will know when you are there. Once there, read aloud each intention as you release the petals in the wind or toss the bark/wood pieces into the wildness around you.

Remain in this silence as long as you like. When you are finished, thank the nature spirits, the universe, and the silence. Above all things, honor and offer gratitude to the generosity of that which made you.

Your ritual is complete.

The Magic of Yoga

Melissa Tipton

When working magic, we often emphasize the mental-spiritual component, such as crafting our intention or focusing on a desired outcome, with the body seen as a vehicle for motoring our mind around the room and carrying out mental directives. However, the body has powerful wisdom and energy of its own, and taking yoga postures (*asanas*) off the mat and into your rituals is a great way to tap into the body's energy. Life in your body is wonderfully unique; unlike mental and spiritual experiences that, to some extent, you can share with others, your physical experience is personal. Thus, it's very important to listen to your body when exploring the following practices. Your body's magic might express itself differently than what I'm proposing here, so trust your gut—literally.

16

There are a number of different ways to incorporate asanas into your magic, and we'll be focusing on three: building energy in ritual, supercharging your intentions, and tapping into higher wisdom prior to divination. We'll also explore how to translate poses not listed here into magical aids so you can customize your physical practice as needed.

Building Energy in Ritual

One way of visualizing the energy-building process is to picture a ball of light emerging from the ground, expanding upward and outward, perhaps in a sphere or cone shape. To translate this into physical postures, we'll focus on poses that start low and expand, mirroring the movement of the energy. Begin in a variation of Child's Pose: Bend your knees and sit back on your heels, then fold forward until your forehead rests on the earth. You have the option to place a bolster or rolled up blanket between your feet to elevate your seat and a bolster under your forehead. If possible, slide your arms back along your sides, palms facing up to emphasize the containment of this pose. Now it's time to build the energy. Feel your intimate connection to the earth, and use your body like a magnet to draw this energy up and into the container of your physical posture. I find it helpful to visualize and feel the energy, but use whatever senses work best for you.

When you feel ready, transition to the next pose. Slide your hands forward and use them to come into tabletop position (hands and wrists directly under shoulders, knees under hips). Feel the four legs of your table containing the energy, which can now expand to fill this larger space. Start to push away the ground with your hands, causing your spine to gently round, giving the energy more room to build. Continue by letting your palms lift, coming up to your fingertips, then releasing your hand contact with the ground as your upper body rolls upward into a kneeling position. Imagine the energy like glowing taffy; your body is pulling it upward, encouraging it to expand.

Bring your palms behind you, like you're sliding them into jean pockets. Push firmly into your glutes with both hands as you lengthen your spine and open your heart. You don't need to fall into a backbend here; really focus on opening your chest by gently pulling your shoulder blades down and together and gently tilting your chin up to open your throat. Be mindful of collapsing into your lower back and stay as vertical as needed to avoid this. Imagine that energy ball expanding, and through the opening of your heart and throat, it starts to build toward the top, creating a cone that's still grounded and fed by the earth.

Drop your chin to a neutral position, return your torso in line above your hips, and then prepare to move again. Come onto your feet, staying low (squat, if that's accessible for you), then roll upward, bit by bit, until you're standing, bringing the energy with you. With your arms at your sides, move them upward like you're creating a standing snow angel, allowing your palms to touch above your head. Through this entire movement, bring the energy along. Feel as new energy swells up from the earth, causing the ball to expand, and help the energy gather into a cone shape with the arms and hands, which come together to shape the point of the cone. You might even clasp fingers and thumbs, except your index fingers, which will point to the sky.

Give yourself a few breaths in this pose, allowing the energy to build to a crescendo (you can even bounce on the balls of your feet, like you're "priming the pump" of the cone, until the energy feels ready to burst) while you focus every fiber of your being on your ritual intention, imbuing the energy with this magical purpose. I like to state my intention three times, followed by "So mote it be," just prior to releasing the energy. When you're ready to release, fling your arms open to the sky, look up, and free the cone of energy. When this feels complete, cross your arms over your chest, palms resting on opposite shoulders, to signify that you are releasing attachment to the energy, giving it full permission to travel as needed to carry out your intention. Sweep your hands diagonally across your torso until the same hand is resting on the same-side

hip, then continue by brushing your hands down the fronts of your thighs, all the way down to the ground, bending your knees as much as necessary, releasing any excess energy, and giving thanks.

Supercharging Intentions

This next sequence of poses I find well suited to magic such as New Moon intention setting. I might not be doing a full-blown ritual and raising a cone of power, but I want to align my energy with a specific outcome. Viewing the movements symbolically, you'll be harnessing your personal energy and tuning it to the frequency of your intention with your focus aimed at the desired results. With a clear intention in mind, begin by standing with your eyes closed, one hand over your heart, the other hand over your belly. Breathe here, focusing on your intention, feeling the energy gathering at your heart and belly centers. Allow the energy to expand, connecting the heart and belly.

Leaving your hands in place, step your feet apart, wider than your hips, feet angled outward (look down and make sure your toes are pointing in the same direction as your knees, adjusting if needed). Bend your knees to lower into a high squat and slowly expand your arms apart to shoulder height, elbows bent at 90 degrees, palms facing forward like goalposts. Bring your awareness to your pelvic bowl, and feel this creative center ignite, joining with the belly and heart, forming a column of energy. Let the energy simultaneously extend in both directions, reaching down through your tailbone into the earth, and out through your crown into the sky. You might feel your spine lengthen with this movement of energy. Take a moment to feel your feet firmly planted, your palms facing forward,

A Little Bit of Magic

THESE EFFECTIVE TECHNIQUES TAP INTO YOUR BODY'S NATURAL POWER AND WISDOM TO ENHANCE YOUR MAGIC.

and your head supported above your center of gravity. Feel your embodiment of the five points of the pentacle and your integration of earth, air, fire, water, and spirit. You have all of these energies available to fuel your intention.

Maintaining your awareness of this energetic column, start to shift: leave your arms in position, come up from the squat, and pivot to your right. Your right foot should be pointing straight forward while your left is pointing out to the side. Adjust the stance as needed until you feel secure, then rotate your ribs until your torso is facing left, coming into a modified Warrior II. The energy might be feeling intense in your arms; if possible, maintain the position

and allow the energy to build (if you need to, relax by placing both hands over your heart and letting your shoulders release). Return your focus to your central energetic column and state your intention. Turn your head to look forward, into the future, and reach your right hand out to the horizon. With your left hand, reach over your left shoulder, like you're trying to pat yourself on the back, and imagine pulling an energetic arrow from a quiver slung on your back. You are drawing some of your energy to direct at your intention. Pull the "arrow" over your head toward your right hand until both palms meet with your fingers pointing straight ahead.

Focus on your intention, looking toward the horizon and imagining yourself already enjoying the desired outcome. Give yourself a few breaths to really soak in this feeling, then start to draw your left hand back, in line with your ear, like you're drawing back a bow string. When you're ready, "fire" the arrow by quickly bringing your right hand forward (optional: create a loud clap by bringing the palms together) and say, "So mote it be!" Come out of the pose and shake off any tension or excess energy.

Poses for Divination

A powerful way to attune before divination is to use gentle movements to acknowledge your connection to divine wisdom. Start in Mountain Pose, feet hip width apart, arms down by your sides. Close your eyes, and take a few moments to scan your body from head to toe, noticing any areas of tension, such as eyebrows, jaw, neck, shoulders, hips, thighs, calves, and feet. If you encounter tension, don't force it away; simply breathe and say inwardly, "Softening." When you're ready to move, on an inhale, slowly circle your arms up from your sides, palms facing up, and imagine the space around you filled with the threads of a glowing web. As you move, you brush these information-laden threads, which connect you to an infinite network of divine wisdom. You might intuitively wiggle your fingers as your arms reach upward, gently strumming the threads.

Bring your palms together above your head and gently look up with eyes closed. Feel your third eye blossom in response to this

rich web of information. Draw your prayer hands down to your third eye, returning your chin to a neutral position, and take a few breaths here. Say inwardly three times, "I receive the information that is correct and good for me at this time." Bring your prayer hands down to your heart and say inwardly three times, "I integrate this information in a way that is correct for me on all levels." If performing divination for someone else, you can substitute, "I communicate this information in a way that is correct and good for (name)."

Start to hinge forward at the hips, bending your knees as much as necessary, releasing your hands to the earth when it feels right. Stay here for a breath and say, "My ego surrenders to perfect love, trust, and wisdom. May this divination be in service of the highest good, harming none. So mote it be." Then, perform your chosen divination.

Adapting Other Poses

There are many ways to incorporate asanas into your magic beyond what we've discussed here. An easy place to start is by looking at the names of poses; they're often descriptive enough to inspire magical uses. For example, poses with animal names, such as Cobra, Crow, Tortoise, and Eagle can be used to commune with animal guides or to introduce their energy or animal medicine to any magical activity. You can also weave this magic into your daily life by going into a specific animal pose prior to, for example, a challenging work presentation or a first date, calling on the power of this animal to guide and support you.

Other poses have object names, such as Boat, Bridge, Gate, and Plow, and these can be explored symbolically. For example, use Boat Pose for travel magic, literal or metaphorical (e.g., leaving an unhealthy relationship or moving toward a goal). Bridge pose can help you make connections (between people, ideas, etc.) or traverse seemingly impassable routes, such as moving through a trying situation to a desired outcome. Gate Pose can support you in establishing healthy boundaries that allow in what you want and need while keeping out what does not serve, and Plow Pose can help you unearth hidden options, ideas, and latent gifts when you feel stuck, or it can prime your energetic soil for planting the seeds of new endeavors.

You can also look at the movements of a pose and, again, view them through a symbolic lens. For example, if you're feeling stuck and constricted, perhaps you start in a bound-up pose. This could be as simple as sitting cross-legged with your arms wrapped around you in a tight hug or more complex, like Eagle Pose, in which your arms and legs are tightly wound. Use this pose to really get in touch with what you're experiencing, allowing any pertinent messages to come through, opening to the lessons of your discomfort. Then, expand into an opening pose of your choice, from lying on your back with arms and legs outstretched, palms open to the sky, or

more advanced poses like Camel or Wheel. Ask for guidance and be open to options and ideas that can help you move into this more expansive state in your day-to-day life. You can browse books and websites for pose ideas (Yoga Journal's online pose finder and *2,100 Asanas: The Complete Yoga Poses* by Daniel Lacerda are two great resources), and play around with how the pose looks, how it feels in your body, and the meaning behind its name or origin to inspire magical uses. Always remember to modify the poses as needed so you're not creating undue strain or any pain in the body.

A Morning Power Boost

The following is a great sequence to do first thing in the morning to prime your energy for the day. Before getting out of bed, bring your knees gently in toward your chest. Only go as far as feels good without straining or forcing. Lightly rock side to side to awaken healthy communication between left and right, receptive and ac-

tive. Reach in between your knees and either hook your big toes with your fingers or grab the outside edges of your feet, and extend your heels toward the ceiling. Leave a generous bend in your knees, and lightly rock side to side, again feeling the connection and balance between left and right.

Release and plant your feet, knees bent, and scooch to the edge of the bed. Start to rock forward and backward, building energy and momentum, then rock powerfully forward, planting your feet on the floor, coming into standing and swinging your arms up to the sky, greeting the day with strength and openness. Bring your hands to prayer at the heart, close your eyes, and contemplate one thing you're grateful for, filling up with gratitude on the inhale and streaming this energy into the world on the exhale. When you're ready, open your eyes and start your day with fresh, sparkling energy!

The Shamanic Mesa

Daniel Moler

I had always wanted to be more connected to nature in my spiritual life.

The usual routine of churches and ceremonies felt too disconnected from what seemed to be a natural spirituality found in the elements that surrounded us every day. Walks and time spent in the wilderness were helpful, but I wanted something deeper. I wanted to incorporate the natural world into my spiritual practice.

I found what I was looking for the first time I met a *curandero* (a shamanic folk healer) who introduced me to his *mesa*. Literally meaning "table" in Spanish, the mesa is an altar where religious rites are performed to gain access and connection to the spiritual world (God, Goddess, Great Spirit, etc.). It can also be used to facilitate healing in yourself or for another person. In a way, it is an access point to the universe: both seen and unseen forces. As noted by shamanic practitioner Matthew Magee, the mesa is "a living control panel, co-created by Spirit and the curandero [shaman], to become a vehicle for experiencing the ineffable." The mesa assists the curandero in diagnosing the cause of issues in life and resolving them.

Originating in Latin America, and most especially Peru, the mesa is used in a variety of ways. Each region, lineage, and family does it a little bit differently. Some mesas are wrapped in a bundle (with sacred objects contained within) and others are laid flat on the ground or a table (where sacred objects are placed on top). There is no one specific way in which a mesa must be used. Many curanderos consider themselves Roman Catholic while still practicing elements of their native heritage. In fact, this synthesis is important as it has evolved the practice of *curanderismo* into a unique blend of traditions and processes that have become inherently cross-cultural in nature.

When I met that curandero for the first time, I committed to being trained in his particular lineage: the Pachakuti Mesa Tradition (PMT). The PMT was brought to the United States by Peruvian curandero don Oscar Miro-Quesada. Eventually, I later came under the direct tutelage of don Oscar and was granted the honor of being a sanctioned teacher in the lineage. The responsibility of a teacher is to bring the medicine of the mesa to the Western world.

Pachakuti is an indigenous Peruvian Quechua term that means "transformation" or, more literally, "turning over the earth." It is the name given to the tilling process the Quechua use before planting their crops. Likewise, it is the name given to the alchemical process one undergoes during apprenticeship into the PMT. The Pachakuti mesa is designed to enact transformation, on both a personal and planetary scale.

As in most shamanic traditions, the Pachakuti mesa is arranged in such a way that it honors the directions of the compass, as well as incorporating a fifth direction as a unifying axis point. Each direction carries with it a collection of elements, archetypes, and attributes that represent the fundamental powers of the natural world. The elements are essential components to understanding shamanic magic and mysticism. As once written by the esoteric adept Franz Bardon, "Everything that has been created came into being through the effects of the elements." This is the key to shamanic magic: tapping into the natural powers of creation to become creators ourselves.

These are directions and elemental attributions of the mesa:

South: The south is called *Pachamama* (Mother Earth), which honors the element of earth. The totemic animal spirit of Pachamama is the boa or anaconda, who lives closest to the ground. This is the place on the mesa for physical healing.

West: The west is called *Mamakilla* (Grandmother Moon), which honors the elements of water. The totemic animal spirit of Mamakilla is the dolphin or whale, who knows best how to navigate the waters of emotion. This is the place on the mesa for healing of the heart.

North: The north is called *Wiracocha* (Creator/Great Spirit), which honors the element of air. The totemic animal spirit of Wiracocha is the eagle or condor, who soars high in the winds of the Creator. This is the place on the mesa for spiritual healing.

East: The east is called *Intitayta* (Father Sun), which honors the element of fire. The totemic animal spirit of Intitayta is the puma or jaguar, who like a flame can see through the darkness with a cutting precision. The is the place on the mesa for healing of the mind.

Center: The center is called *K'yuchi* (rainbow), which honors the element of ether. The totemic animal spirit of K'yuchi is the llama or alpaca, who is an animal of service in the Andes, which emulates the prime virtue of shamanic healing. This is the place on the mesa for healing of the soul.

These areas of the mesa are fields of power that exist naturally in the world around us. They can be harnessed and utilized, specifically through the mesa itself, to facilitate the healing faculties of each elemental function. They are all parts of a collective, a compass that can guide humanity to a path of self-empowerment. Indigenous knowledge has understood this for thousands of years, but it is an understanding that has been lost in our modern way of life. Yet, the objective of the PMT is to ensure every citizen of humanity has access to this ancient, spiritual technology.

Building Your Mesa

Shamanism is an art. All artforms require a certain amount of training to establish a framework, but then it is incumbent on the artist to allow their intuition to guide their creative flow.

The mesa should be treated no differently. Learn the basics, and then make the mesa yours. In shamanism, tradition is important, but individuality is encouraged. It is your connection to the spirit world that matters, not the ideology of a dogma or guru.

The mesa is home to an abundance of ritual objects. These objects are called *artes*, which is Spanish for "arts" or "artifices," thus immediately implying that this altar and the artifacts within are a result of your creative process.

The first step to building a mesa is to acquire a sacred blanket or cloth to act as the base of your altar. In the PMT, Peruvian textiles are normally used for their thick and endurable fibers that provide a steady palate for ritual objects to be placed. What is most important is to use something important to you, a cloth that resonates with your spiritual paradigm. I have seen some mesa carriers use cloths with designs that are Celtic, Native American, and so on. Find something with which you are comfortable being the foundation of the "control panel" that you will be using to navigate the powers of the elements.

Once you have found your cloth, you will then want to acquire artes to make up the primary directional schema of the mesa itself. As each direction expresses an elemental aspect of the universe, you will seek an arte to represent that designation:

A LITTLE BIT OF MAGIC

By connecting with these ancient ways, it is the shamanic worldview that human beings will develop an awareness of right relationship with each other and the planet we live on.

South/Pachamama: A stone, crystal, or other artifact that will represent Mother Earth and the material expression of life.

West/Mamakilla: A shell, bowl of water, or other artifact that will represent the waters of the planet and the realm of emotion.

North/Wiracocha: A feather to represent the element of air and spiritual world. It is a good idea acquire a small vase or container to fill with sand in which you can stand up your feather (so as to avoid any wind interference).

East/Intitayta: A single white candle to represent the purity of fire and the clarity of a pristine mind.

Center/K'yuchi: Your most sacred object that best represents your spiritual path, expressing the etheric realm of your soul coming into its fruition.

Selecting the right artes for your mesa should not be a frivolous endeavor. Take your time and acquire them based upon your intuition, your inner guidance of what feels in alignment with your

mind, heart, and body. Take a walk out in nature. Ask Creator to send these artes your way. Clear your senses and allow these items to come to you as naturally as possible, rather than forcing the process. Whether they can be found in the wilderness, in a metaphysical book shop, or even a flea market, the universe will deliver what we need as long as we stay open to receive. Keep your mind and heart open.

Consecrating Your Sacred Space

Before setting up your mesa, locate a space within your home that can be reserved specifically for sacred ceremony. Some people will have a separate room, an out building, or even a space within their bedroom. Regardless of where it is, this is a space you will use only for your shamanic work of connection with the powers of the mesa.

When your space is selected, you will want to orient the mesa so that you can sit to the south of the altar space. This way you are always looking north, toward Creator.

Consecrating your ground before setting out your altar is important. It is a declaration of your intention to the land in which you reside—and all the spirits that occupy it—that you are creating a sacred space. It is also an offering, a ritual feeding that will satiate the unseen powers of the earth. This is not just a ceremonial protocol. Building, consecrating, and then activating your mesa can itself be a meditative or healing process, connecting you with these elemental powers and their healing capacities to help influence your life. Submit to these processes as healing endeavors, allowing the energy of each direction to flow into your consciousness and envelop your physical, emotional, spiritual, and mental bodies.

First, burning sage or palo santo wood is a good way to cleanse any dense or negative energy from the area. The smoke of these essences is known in indigenous traditions to ward off any unwanted influences and open a new space for growth and rejuvenation. Then, follow these simple steps to consecrate your ground:

1. Offer a few drops of *agua de florida* (flower water) to the center of the ground in which you will be placing your mesa. This water is meant to satisfy Pachamama's thirst in gratitude for all she has offered us as her children.

2. Offer some cornmeal, drawing a circle around that central point you offered the agua de florida. Start in the south and draw the circle clockwise. This represents the sacred hoop of life, that all things are connected in an infinite cycle of time and space.

3. Offer some tobacco, drawing a line from the northern tip of your cornmeal circle to the south, then from the east to the west. This is to symbolize that the infinity of the circle becomes squared within our human understanding of space-time, that the sun rises and sets from our microcosmic perspective, and life has a finite beginning and end.

4. Finally, acquire three bay or rose leaves (in Peru coca is typically used) to offer a *k'intu*. A *k'intu* is a ritual offering used via the healing power of a plant, married with the breath of the practitioner, to create a union between human and prayer. The number three is important in many mystery traditions. It is generally considered to represent the three shamanic worlds of existence (upper, middle, and lower) but can also be used to represent the three attributes of shamanic service: love, wisdom, and hard work. Blow a prayer of intention to embody these three attributes and then place the *k'intu* in the center of the circled cross you created. Seal your consecration with a snap of your fingers, symbolizing your completion of the consecration ceremony.

Activating Your Mesa

Be sure to cleanse all your ritual objects before constructing your mesa space and laying your cloth. Again, sage or palo santo is a satisfactory tool for this task. Then, you will lay your sacred cloth down over your consecration. The groundwork is set. You are ready to activate your artes and thus the entire mesa itself.

Activating each arte before placing it on the designated space of your mesa is vital to accessing and securing the aim of each ritual object. In all magical work, your will and intention are above all else the canvas on which the imagination can manifest a new reality. So, as with anything placed on a sacred altar, take some time to activate each individual arte.

Still seated, start at the south of your mesa and work clockwise to the west, then north and east, and finally end your activation in the center. Place the Pachamama arte you acquired in your right hand and open your left palm turned upward to the heavens. Close your eyes and relax your body, breathing comfortably in a steady rhythm. Clear your mind of all thought, opening yourself to the emptiness of a meditative state. When you feel sufficiently clear of all distraction, bring into focus this visualization using the pure power of your imagination:

1. Imagine a shaft of light coming down from the heavens above and pouring over your body. Feel this light as the power of creation itself, seeding your intention with the backing of Creator.

2. Open your crown, allowing yourself to be filled completely with this essence. You can imagine your crown to be a lotus flower blossoming to drink the light of the sun, its life-giving nourishment infusing your body.

3. Receiving this light also in your left palm, feel the light rush through your left arm, into your heart space, and then down through your right arm into the arte in your right hand. Through this passageway you will turn the life-giving light from the heavens into a specific intention to embody within the specific arte. For Pachamama, you will of course call in all the elemental power of the earth, the totem of the boa or anaconda, as well as the capacity to invoke physical healing. Spend a few minutes drawing forth the fullest potential for the powers of this direction into the arte.

4. Intone "Pachamama" seven times to permanently seal this essence into arte. Seven is another powerful number to use in magical work; as a holy number, it is used to gain sanction from the higher powers. Allow your intonation to be slow and low, using the vibration as a mantra to both enliven you with physical restoration and also to call forth the nature of the arte's new purpose as a healing artifact.

5. When finished, bring the arte to your lips and blow a final prayer of intention into it. Place it in its designated section on the mesa and snap your fingers in completion.

6. Complete this process again for the other directions. You will of course change the healing powers for each direction based upon the elemental force as explained earlier.

Incorporate your own understanding of these powers into your activation process. Without your personal flavor of spirituality, the mesa will become a stagnant tool without any life. So, feel free to incorporate spiritual practices and interests that suit your alignment with Creator. Remember, mesa traditions have evolved through a history of synthetization, different cultures merging to create something new and unique. This is how shamanic and folk traditions have survived the tests of time. Evolution is key to the inherent purpose of the Pachauti mesa, especially transformation.

Using Your Mesa

The mesa is a reflection of your own soul, a realization of your life path. It is only as effective as your ability to use it, to trust it, and to build a regular practice in which a relationship is grown and maintained like tending a garden. There are two ways in which you can use the artes on your mesa to call forth the elemental powers contained in the respective directions.

The first is *limpias*, ritual clearing of dense or negative energy. This can be accomplished by taking the respective arte and brushing downward over the body, asking the arte to disperse the specific ailment you are trying to alleviate. For instance, if you are dealing with an emotional issue, use your Mamakilla arte to brush away any negative energy affecting your ability stay balanced emotionally. Allow that energy to be collected in the arte as it passes through your body. Blow that excess energy into the earth, trusting that the soil will dissolve it, compost it, and later turn it into life-giving nourishment for new growth.

The second is *floreciendos*, ritual raising of empowerment. This can be accomplished by taking the respective arte and brushing it upward over the body, asking the arte to impart its healing potency. For instance, if you need to bring forth more wisdom and clarity of mind into your life, the Intitayta arte would be a sufficient medicine to bring forward for such a case. Another way to imbue the medicine of the arte is to just hold it in your left hand and draw forth its power from your left palm, letting it flow throughout your body and into any areas with a specific need.

Working with the mesa can be as simple as you want it to be. Curanderos have spent thousands of years using the mesa and re-

fining its potential. Again, it is an art form. You are the creator of the magic you wish to bring forward. The more you experiment and have fun with the mesa's myriad powers, the more skilled you will become. Do your rituals, enjoy the communion with the unseen, and—above all—give thanks to the mesa after every endeavor. Gratitude is the currency of the sacred. Shamanic power grows the more you gain a rapport with the elemental powers of nature.

Growing Your Mesa

I have used a mesa in my spiritual practice for well over a decade now. I started as a person who was lost and confused, insecure in his own process of connecting with Spirit. Growing up in the Midwest, I was raised in a very conservative religious mindset. Guilt and fear were the driving factors of spiritual service, a bewildering ethos for any young mind to handle. In that malaise of spiritual disorientation, I could not find a solid foundation for my life in general, let alone a spiritual one.

Over time, I have grown with the mesa, just as the mesa has grown with me. Mesas change throughout the years, as they should. The mesa, at the end of the day, is a mirror. As I used my mesa to move through my periods of confusion and insecurity—via limpias and floreciendos—things began to evolve. I was able to see how the mesa is nothing but a reflection of my own soul. As my mesa grew in size, accumulating artes with a specific spiritual purpose, I added them in alignment with the elemental powers in which they belonged. Adjustments were made many times, but eventually I found a flow between myself and the unseen realms, a direct interaction and exchange that manifested as a language only I can understand. Every person has their own interpersonal flow. Conversely, every mesa can tap into that flow with you. We are social beings and our ability to understand reality only comes through a participation with other beings.

The mesa is a living, breathing looking glass into your own sense of self. Through the mesa, I have come into my own as a spiritual adept. Not because I am better than anyone else or claim to have some unique spiritual power, but because the mesa has allowed me the ability to see inside myself, manage the attributes of my personality (physical, emotional, spiritual, and mental), and find a sense of security on my life path. This foundation is imperative for any spiritual endeavor. These elemental attributes apply to every human being alive on the planet, regardless of gender, race, or ethnicity. Through the navigational capacities of the mesa as an altar of the soul, I found my orientation in this world and achieved a balance that works best for me.

Resources

Bardon, Franz. *Initiation into Hermetics.* Translated by Gerhard Hanswille and Franca Gallo. Holladay, UT: Merkur Publishing, 1999. Page 25.

Magee, Matthew. *Peruvian Shamanism: The Pachakúti Mesa.* Kearney, NE: Morris Publishing, 2005. Page xvi.

Sacrifice:
In Service of the Gods

Kerri Connor

One of the greatest differences between Pagans today and our ancestors has to do with the concept of sacrifice. Many religions the world over practiced some sort of sacrifice to their gods—whether it be the firsts or best of a harvest, animal sacrifice, or, yes, in some cases even human sacrifice.

This isn't something Pagans don't do anymore. Human sacrifice is completely out of the question. Animal sacrifice may still happen in a few sects, but there are also those who raise their own animals for food, and this can be a part of animal sacrifice in a sense. I'm sure a few also still sacrifice from gardens or crops. But these offerings aren't the norm.

Sacrificing food in our current environment also isn't quite the same as what it was in more ancient times either. Most of us don't have to worry about where our next meal is coming from, so the food-related sacrifices we do make aren't necessarily coming from the deepest sense of giving. Though we all need food to survive, it is not as precious to most of our society as it was hundreds of years ago because it is not as rare or in short supply.

In our current era, time is a commodity. Time is what is precious and valued in our local communities. So then, wouldn't the giving of our time be a greater sacrifice? Giving of your time is not only a sacrifice, but it is also one that can bring with it bountiful rewards. I am talking about the act of volunteering.

While we can devote hours a week to meditations, spells, trance work, and rituals, all those practices often have ourselves as the main benefactor. What better way is there to serve our lords and ladies than to perform service in their names? While we give of our time and possibly talents, we can work to make the earth, and our individual communities, a better place to live.

Many Pagans are earth conscious and follow the "reduce, reuse, recycle" code, but we can take it so much further than that. We can organize neighborhood and highway cleanups. We can host recycling events. We can volunteer in groups to help clean up local parks, waterways, and conservation districts. We can offer classes based on our skills to county and local park districts. We can plan, implement, and help maintain community gardens. All these ideas honor Mother Earth herself while fulfilling a sacrifice of time and aiding the local community. It doesn't hurt that it may give you a huge feeling of accomplishment or gratitude either.

Another natural area for Pagans to gravitate toward when thinking of giving back to the community is working with animals. This may mean volunteering at a shelter, holding a fundraiser, making toys for the animals, organizing food drives, or even becoming a foster family for an animal in need. While local pet shelters always need help, there are places that may house more exotic animals. Rescues exist for wild, farm, and zoo animals, and they all tend to need help too.

Service as a Group

Don't feel you have to limit yourself to these areas though! What interests you? How can you best give? I run the Gathering Grove—we are an eclectic mix, but we do what we can to support each other. One of my passions is helping the homeless. We participated in the fundraiser SleepOut for Shelter for many years, camping out all night in 45-degree temperatures for donations. We collect hats, scarves, gloves, mittens, and yarn (which I then use to knit hats and scarves) to be passed out at a local winter overnight shelter. This shelter is also a Catholic Church that we do laundry for once a month for the shelter bedding. We have helped provide food for lunches and toiletry supplies along with holding a coat drive at a local New Age store.

We've also been known to jump into a frozen lake in northern Illinois in February for the Special Olympics Polar Plunge.

We used to run and sit on the board for a charity named Nurturing Necessities. Our mission was to provide mothers and babies with clothing, toys, diapers, and other necessities to help alleviate financial issues. We would run an annual Halloween scavenger hunt and two metaphysical fairs a year as fundraisers. Unfortunately, when I was diagnosed with breast cancer, we needed to close the organization down.

Even if you don't have a group, you can dedicate your own solo volunteerism to your own deities. But don't let that mean you miss out on doing work with groups too. Use your resources (whether that be social media and other websites or even a sign at a local metaphysical store) to find other Pagans in your area and set up one-time volunteer events. If your group works well together, you may want to consider meeting up several times a year to perform service projects, perhaps one to coincide with each sabbat or Full Moon. Each project can be for the same or different agencies, and it can be detailed to fit with the time of year or theme of the sabbat or can be something that corresponds with the Full Moon. You can check with your local United Way to see if there are opportunities in the area or come up with an idea on your own. Bringing Pagans from different pathways and traditions together to work for a common goal—this is how we change our world for the better.

Pagan Volunteerism

Not only does Pagan volunteerism serve the function of a sacrifice, not only does it better the community, not only does it give us a sense of self-respect and pride when we do a job well done, but it puts Paganism in a positive light for the community to see. Plenty of churches do service in the name of their lord. It's time we put serious effort into doing the same.

No, you don't have to shout from the rooftops that you are a Pagan or Pagan group working on a service project, but imagine the peace you will feel if you don't hide it either. You are doing good for your community. It's okay for people to know Pagans believe in making their world a better place by working for it. After all, if we are stewards and protectors of the earth, perhaps we should be the ones leading the way.

Bringing people together in groups to perform service projects is its own special type of bonding. Sometimes the project is fun and uplifting. Sometimes you might be providing aid to people who have been devasted, such as by cleaning up after a wildfire, tornado, or storm. This creates an entirely different bond to the group you work with, and while you might not ever work with the same group again, you will always have the bond of sharing the experience together.

A Ritual for New Service Projects

If you have a group that practices together and can volunteer together, that is great—but whether you come group-ready or need to create a group for a service project, you should start your project off with an opening ritual.

This ritual is suitable for mixed groups to perform together, as it is generic in nature to deities referenced.

You don't need a high priest or priestess for this ritual, as you can each act as your own. If the group would like to call in elements, watchtowers, or any other aspect of spirit, go ahead and do so. If anyone wants to do a personal dedication or smudging, they should do so at this time as well.

Next bring the group together in a circle and hold your arms out to your sides, touching palms with the person next to you.

Go around the circle clockwise and have each person say,

Palm to palm,
I pass the power.

Once it gets back to the beginning, drop your arms and take three steps (the smaller the group the smaller the steps, the larger the group the larger the steps) in toward the group's center. Clasp hands with the people at your sides. All say,

We come together today from different paths
To honor each our own,
To give of ourselves
To each other and to our community.
We bind together as one to serve our purpose and our deities.
May we recognize and appreciate the love and spirit inside one another.

Allow for a moment of heads bowed in quiet reflection or meditation. When everyone is ready (shown by the lifting of their heads), all say,

Let us go forth and flourish,
Our goal to be achieved.
We are the charge and the change.
Our wish
So mote it be.

This ritual is short enough you can write it down on large dry-erase boards or poster boards and place them on easels for group members to be able to read from during the ritual. (Take pride in these; decorate them up and make them look good—especially if there is a chance the public will see. Let's show them our best!) If your group decides to form into a more permanent structure, you will soon find yourselves memorizing it anyway.

After your service project is done, bring the group back together for a closing. Again, join together in a circle and hold hands. Let anyone who has anything they would like to say about the project speak. This is a time to give personal insights on feelings about the project, such as what was accomplished and positives of working together. This is not a time to complain. It is for positive comments and affirmations only. It's for giving and accepting kudos from one

another. This process also allows people to let out some excess energy and ground a bit.

After everyone has had the opportunity to speak if they wish, end your project with the time-honored phrase:

Merry meet and merry part and merry meet again!

If you are like the Gathering Grove, you may want to add in a bit of whooping and hollering with raised arms to send that last burst of energy off into the universe.

Everyday Boundary Magic and Psychic Protection

Danielle Blackwood

P sychic attack comes in many different forms. And while magickal people know that sometimes this can originate in the spirit world (and occasionally from other practitioners), psychic attack can also come in the insidious form of interactions in everyday life, including through social media. The effects of everyday psychic attack can have just as much of a tangible impact as a curse or a hex. You may feel compromised. You may feel diminished in your power and ability to defend yourself. It can trigger old debilitating feelings from the past that have a real-world effect in the present. You might even feel physically unwell.

While magick, astrology, and various spiritual practices used to be the province of the serious seeker, or adept, the internet has brought a surge in popularity to these and other practices that is a double-edged sword. While the internet brings awareness and knowledge of what was previously hidden and connects us to some brilliant authors, thinkers, and practitioners, it also brings a glut of market-savvy, self-styled priestesses, shamans, and magical practitioners of every stripe. There is a shadow side of social media in the magical/spiritual world that is rife with competition, and the kind of narcissism that is often concurrent with personal branding. There are hierarchies and cliques that preach inclusivity but are anything but inclusive. I found this out firsthand when my book, *The Twelve Faces of the Goddess,* came out in 2018.

When my first book was finally birthed into the world, I was over the proverbial moon. I had managed to distill decades of study, work, and hard-won life experience into words available for anyone to read. To say it was a dream come true is an understatement. Although authors are cautioned not to read their reviews, I'm only

human, and I was filled to overflowing with gratitude as I obsessively checked the various review sites to read the kind and supportive words of my readers. I felt a growing sense of standing in my power, as well as belonging to a community.

However, before long, with the increasing visibility of my work in the world, I began to notice another kind of energy surfacing, specifically from aspiring magickal/spiritual practitioners in a nearby city. As I reached out to some of these other practitioners for connection, both online and off, I felt an inexplicable yet distinct chilliness. And while everyone is entitled to a bad day, this felt different. At first, I thought it was just my imagination. I tried harder. I was friendlier and tried to court these women despite them giving me the cold shoulder. Their rejection triggered feelings I hadn't experienced since I was a teenager. Many who walk the path of Witch know all too well the feeling of being outcast, and although I have done years of my own work, had just had my first book published, and consider myself a pretty confident person, I felt their dismissal as keenly as I did when I was fourteen.

I returned from a successful and celebratory book launch to find that I had my first online troll. And while no author wants to see a negative review of their hard work, this was not simply critical feedback. I realize that not everyone will love my book, or any book for that matter, but the unkind words of the "reviewer" had all the marks of a full-on attack. Checking the other review sites, I saw that she posted on several of them, albeit slightly reworded. Although the posts were anonymous, the reviewer unwittingly left several clues that pointed directly toward someone in one of the nearby online groups. I was floored. My first reaction was disbelief. Why would anyone do this? I could literally feel the negative energy pointed in my direction, and for a brief time the shock that someone I didn't even know would go out of their way to cause me harm destabilized my equilibrium (which is probably precisely the intended outcome of the attack).

Lessons in Psychic Protection

Although I have been a Witch for several decades and have practiced magickal protection at different junctures in my life, since I became an author I have learned some useful new lessons about everyday boundary work and psychic protection that I would like to share.

1. As you grow into your power and become more visible, your boundaries will be tested.

You will know when you are stepping into your power because some people will perceive you as a threat. Unfortunately, it goes with the territory. The brighter you shine, the more some will project the shadow of their own unlived dreams on you. Some will think, "Why her/him? Why not me?" In their discontent with themselves, they may lash out with gossip or worse. Walk with integrity and consider the Witches who came before you. Although they were usually powerful, knowledgeable, and skilled, many were also reviled, rejected and punished because of their power. As you grow into your own power, hold your head up high and be above reproach.

Exercise: As a person coming into your power, how can you maintain your integrity and remain above the projections of other's shadow selves?

2. Insecure people are often unconsciously jockeying for position.

Have you ever met someone with your heart open, wanting to make a connection, only to be rebuffed by a chilly or dismissive response? This is everyday energy work afoot. Despite any appearances to the contrary, the person in question is usually insecure and feels threatened. This is a tactic for getting the upper hand and maintaining a false sense of status. The silent message is "you are not important" or "I'm so important that I don't have time for you." The person may not even consciously realize they are coming off this way, but for whatever reason, they are feeling the need to inflate themselves in your presence.

On the flip side, have you encountered someone and immediately felt a clean and clear welcome from their greeting? The more centered a person is in what they do and who they are, usually the kinder and more generous of their time and spirit they are to others. As a first-time author, it was daunting for me to reach out to accomplished and well-known public figures with my manuscript in hand, asking if they would take the time to read it. I braced myself for their rejection every time I hit send. These authors were overwhelmingly gracious and giving of their time and energy. I was occasionally moved to tears by their generosity, supportive words, and kindness. Be mindful of the company you seek and keep.

Exercise: Describe when you have experienced these two different types of energy. Who lifts you up and why?

3. Are you giving your power away for approval?

If you find yourself with someone in a position that feels distinctly like an earlier experience in which you gave away your power, you might be triggered by an energetic power play. If this happens, stop. Step back energetically and physically. Call your energy back, and ground and center on the spot. Shield yourself if necessary.

Resist the temptation to try harder to get the other person to "like you." You will not gain approval from this person by further giving yourself away. They are playing an energy game to boost their own ego: the silent message is that you need them, but they don't need you. Change your body language immediately and reserve your energy. Place your hand over your solar plexus. This kind of exchange can occur face to face or online.

Exercise: Write about a time that you have given your power away in order to gain someone's approval or validation. How did it make you feel? Were you conscious of your own underlying motives?

4. Creating boundaries may be uncomfortable.

Most of us have trouble creating and maintaining healthy boundaries in all situations. Boundaries take practice. It may feel difficult to say no at work. Or maybe it's hard to keep good boundaries with a particular family member. When you start creating stronger boundaries, some people will push back. They may become angry or withdraw, causing you to feel guilty and want to give in or make an exception. It takes strength and personal conviction to maintain healthy boundaries. It also requires a fearless personal inventory to ascertain what is truly important to you. Some people will push or overstep your boundaries, forcing you to stand even deeper in your power. This can be easier said than done. Keep practicing.

Exercise: How do you know when your boundaries have been crossed?

5. Connect with your allies.

Working with deities connected to boundaries and sovereignty can be very helpful in everyday magical protection. Call on Macha, the Irish sovereignty goddess who is associated with creating strong boundaries and standing one's ground. Or call on Mars, who was originally a protector of farmers, fields, and boundaries. Allies from the mineral kingdom can also be used for protection: black tourmaline, hematite, smoky quartz, obsidian, and onyx work well. Jet is said to be a particularly strong Witch's ally and protects against psychic attack. It is especially helpful on the bedside table to protect against bad dreams and negative energies while you are sleeping.

Plant allies are also very useful, and protective herbs can be dried and made into a sachet or powder and used as a protection amulet or sprinkled at windows and doorways around your home. Although many are familiar with sage and palo santo for their cleansing and protective properties, the following protective and purifying blend is one of the most potent I have used. For best results, grow your own herbs or find the yarrow and hyssop at a herb farm. If you can obtain the herbs in flower, they are at their most potent. Gather the cedar or Douglas fir ethically, taking care not to damage any trees. Be sure to thank the tree for what you have taken. Crafting this protective smudge is best done when the Moon is in its last quarter or when it is in Aries or Scorpio.

Exercise: Make a list of your personal allies.

Psychic Protection Bundle

You will need:

Black candle

Inkless ballpoint pen or other similar implement

Working surface, such as a table

Plant allies: equal parts fresh cedar or Douglas fir, yarrow, and
hyssop

Black embroidery thread

Cleanse and consecrate your working area. Ground and center in
your preferred way. Inscribe a protective sigil on the candle with
the pen (pentacle, Mars symbol, etc.). Light the candle and invoke
a protective deity that you are drawn to. (Note: it is extremely useful to do some research and connect with the qualities of your chosen deity beforehand.) Ask for their help as you set your intention
for protection. Dedicate your creation in their name. Walk with the
lit black candle counterclockwise around your table, and say (for
example):

I hereby light this candle in honor of the goddess Macha,
Great Queen of boundaries, protection, and sovereignty.
Help me stand fully in my power, and mark my boundaries here and now.
No one and nothing that means me harm may cross.

Set the candle safely on the table and allow it to burn while you do your work.

Sort each plant ally into three little piles, meditating on and connecting with the qualities of each. Leave some space immediately before you so you can assemble your bundle.

Place several small cedar branches (between five and twelve inches long) in front of you. On top of the cedar, layer the yarrow and finally the hyssop. Gather the plants in your hand and begin wrapping the embroidery thread from the bottom up. You may have to spiral down again, making sure to pull the thread as tight as you can. As you are wrapping your bundle, visualize your intent of protection. Ask the plants to be your allies in this work. Finish by tying a secure double knot. Thank the deity and the plant allies that you are working with. Allow the candle to burn out safely, or extinguish the flame with a candlesnuffer. Don't worry if you have a few bits and pieces sticking out of your bundle. You can trim these later if you wish.

Place your newly created bundle in a cool, dry place and allow it to dry for several days. As soon as it is dry, your smudge is ready to use. You can now light it and use the smoke to cleanse and protect yourself or your space whenever you feel the need.

Magic for Moving to a New Place

Divina Cornick

There's an art to moving. It's a strange blend of magic that brings together the thrill of the unknown and the sadness of leaving behind everything you know. You are quite literally trying to transplant yourself, the life you have made, the identity you have forged, into a new environment. Think of yourself as a plant. Maybe you've tested the soil and are certain the pH levels are exactly what you need, or perhaps you are going to plant some random seeds to see what sprouts. Sometimes you take root super fast, and sometimes you find yourself moving again a few months later because you weren't able to get enough sun and nourishment.

Either way, change is good for the soul.

Moving the furniture around your house stirs up everything that's been left to sit and dwell. Moving your body, whether on your yoga mat or in a dance, does the same thing and shakes up any emotions or energies that have gotten stagnant or are clinging to your mind and tissues. Movement clears the air and makes room for new opportunities, experiences, and relationships.

Growing up, I moved a lot. I swear I have never lived in any one place for more than four years. No, I wasn't an army brat. I just have a mom who is a double Sag (Sagittarius Sun sign *and* ascending sign). Most of the time, I didn't have a choice in the matter. I was too young to have a vote. My mom would just tell me what was going on and I had to respond in suit, picking the toys and clothes that meant the most to me and mourning over what didn't fit in the car. I learned very early on what was important and what didn't really matter, even though the object might have been pretty and part of me was sad to let it go.

We moved to find new adventures, sometimes with no warning or any planning at all. Mom wanted a change of scenery or a new job. Sometimes we moved for love, and sometimes it was because the old life had become overwhelming for a single mom. I grew accustomed to free-flowing energy, never being tied down. I became addicted to the quest for something new.

But, no matter why we move or how far away from our last place, it's important to understand that we always take our problems with us: We are who we are no matter where we are. (Say that five times fast—it'll be funny, but it's also true.)

Moving is good for the soul. Change is life. Once we stop moving and changing, evolving and growing, we are no longer living. However, moving will never make any of our problems disappear.

But, magic can totally help!

Magical Moving Rules

Normally, I never say never, but some rules are there for a reason. Here are some of my tried and true magical practices for making my moves smooth and successful:

Declutter

I never take everything with me. I go through every pair of socks and every book, and, just like when I was a kid, I consciously decide what I want to bring with me and what I need to say goodbye to. This goes for physical things as well as mindsets and behaviors. Even if I only donate a small bag of things or throw away a single sock that I can't find the mate to, I know I am actively clearing out the old to make way for something new, something better.

Leave the Vacuum or Broom at Your Old Place

Think about it. You sucked up months or years worth of dust, dirt, and all sorts of other disgusting things into that vacuum cleaner (or picked it up with your dust pan). I don't care if you emptied the bag. That machine is marred for life. Do you really want to take that energy or even physical dirt into your new home? Energetically, you want your move to signify a clean slate. That deserves some new cleaning supplies. The first things I buy whenever I move into a new place is a new broom, vacuum, and kitchen sponge.

Wash Your New Door

Fill up a bucket with warm water and sprinkle in some salt, a handful of dried rosemar,y and a few drops of lemon juice. The salt is to purify, the rosemary is to protect, and the lemon is for prosperity. Take a washcloth and just go to town, wiping down the door on both sides. This is cleaning away any old energy clinging to the house and ensuring that only good vibes can enter.

A Ritual to Bless Your Old Place

I think it's important to be grateful for every step we take in life. Every step forward is possible because of the ground that caught us on the step before.

This ritual will clear the air and create space for the next tenant. It will cast out all negativity and bless the apartment or house for whoever is taking up residence after you leave. It will also cut the cords that connect you so you are free to move on.

The spell is done at the witching hour, so you might like to do this ritual on the midnight before you move out. However, if that's not possible, in the spoken portion you can swap "the witching hour" to "this magical hour" because *all* hours have the potential to be magical (*wink*).

You will need:
Selenite wand
Drum, tambourine, or some kind of noisemaker
A song that makes you want to dance (I'm partial to Florence and
   the Machine's "Shake It Out")
White candles

Prepare by placing a candle in each direction, either in a window-sill or on the floor.

The first order of business is to clear the air. Moving is a fresh start for everyone involved. That means you and for people who will be moving into your home after you've left. You want to make sure you are clearing out your own energy to make room for theirs. Also, cutting the cords, the ties that bind you to people and places, will keep you healthy and grounded in the present.

Before anything else can happen, you want to clear out your energy from the space. So, put on your favorite dancing song, pick up

A LITTLE BIT OF MAGIC

Make time to bless your old place. It's tempting to move on without looking back, but it's good karma to bless the place you're leaving behind.

your noisemaker, and begin your dance around your house. Make as much noise as you want and have fun with it. Act as though you are herding the energy to one area of the house and "chase" it out with sound and motions from your arms and body.

To begin the ritual, use your selenite wand to draw your circle. Make it as big as your place. Walk through every room of your apartment or house three times, making the whole place part of your ritual.

Once your circle is made, stand facing the north, arms at your side with your palms facing forward. Say,

On this night, at the witching hour,
I call upon the divine power.
Stand with me, in this sacred space;
Bless it now with love and grace.

Light the candle in north. Keeping your palms open, turn to face the east. Say,

Powerful wind and gentle breeze,
Bless this space with peace and ease.

Light the candle in east. Keeping your palms open, turn to face the south. Say,

Fierce flame and brilliant light,
Cleanse this space and make it bright.

Light the candle in south. Keeping your palms open, turn to face the west. Say,

Healing waters that ebb and flow,
May the good vibes take root and grow.

Light the candle in west. Stand in the center of the space you spent the most time, whether that was the kitchen, bedroom, living room, and so on. Open your arms wide and say,

Before I leave, let me be clear:
This has been a blessed year.
Thank you for your safe, loving embrace.
I am truly grateful to have lived in this place.
Please welcome those who come after me.
As I will, so mote it be.

Extinguish the candles and draw a pentacle in the smoke above them.

Then, turn to your front door and bow your head. Forgive what wasn't perfect and be grateful for what helped you. Honor the space and send it love, so that it might bless the next tenant with more of the good things it has to offer. You can leave the candles in a drawer for the next owner. I like to think that those candles will help their future owner if the power ever goes out and they are in need of some light.

Walk around your place counterclockwise, drawing up the circle into your selenite wand.

I always end my rituals by saying,

The circle is open but never broken.

Be sure to set the selenite wand in the sun for three days after, letting it cleanse and recharge in the light.

A Shorter Blessing

Even with the list of rules, don't take any of it so seriously that it stresses you out. Magic is in the intention. If you don't have time or the freedom to sage the whole house, whisper a blessing to the front door. Say,

May all who enter be happy and prosperous.

It can be that simple.

If you're building your own house, you can write spells and mantras in the studs, weaving magic into the very foundation.

If you're moving into a brand-new place, you can make sure all the floors are swept before a single box is brought inside.

When I moved in with my boyfriend and his roommate, my boyfriend did the initial cleaning. He swept and uncluttered his closet, and then I followed him with a burning bundle of sage. On my first real night living there we made homemade pizzas and our roommate played a song on his guitar. The next morning we toasted the move with mimosas. It was something simple and not overly spiritual, because I am the only Pagan, but it was beautiful and full of our good intentions.

Home Is Where the Heart Is

Having moved so much, I understand more than most that home is truly where the heart is (or where your dogs are). Your home, your hearth, is the center of everything, just as the heart is the center chakra, bringing together the cosmic and earthly powers. The vibration it carries, the feeling the space gives you, effects everything from how good your sex life is to how you're treated at work. If you feel safe and confident at home, that will go with you everywhere.

Air Magic

The Intent of Intention

Charlynn Walls

The most powerful spells or rites come from an absolute conviction in our ability to effect change in our lives coupled with the intent of what we want to accomplish. One of the most powerful, and yet simplest, spells for me ended up being putting myself out to the universe for a new and lasting love. I do not find love spells to be all that effective when directed at a particular person. However, I was ready to move on from the state of my love life at the time. It was stagnant and I was ready to break through and move ahead. I wanted to bring into my life a person who was like and yet unlike those I had been with in recent relationships. So, I did not envision any particular person; instead I envisioned someone who would fit with me, my goals, and someone who, like myself, was in it for the long haul.

I spent a lot of time and thought into manifesting my intention. I tend to be a list person, so I would make lists about things that I needed to accomplish. Obviously, in this case I was tending to a love spell and created a list of attributes that I wanted to see in a potential partner. I did not want to influence a specific person, but I sought to draw to myself a specific type of person. I contemplated what I wanted in a significant other, what was important to me in another person. I did not focus on only physical attributes but those that dealt with emotions and the spiritual as well. I wanted someone who would complement my life choices but also someone who would challenge me.

I constructed my spell out of putting my intention out into the universe and was fortunate to find someone whom I had a true connection with. Someone who fit my ideals. I also utilized the correspondences for my type of spell. This included the timing of the spell, the tools to accompany it, and any other natural items that I might desire.

While my spell did not manifest into reality immediately, I could see it shift my perspective. I was more thoughtful in the dates that I chose. It also brought someone back into my life who I had thought was long gone. This was an individual I thought I would never see again, and yet this is the person who truly complimented and supported me. I eventually married him, and we are still married!

Is Intent Important?

In short, yes! Intention is extremely important to the creation of a well-rounded spell that can produce desired results. Intent gives a direction for the spell or ritual and it draws to it the components that will support it.

A spell or rite is composed of several elements. You have the tools, the timing, and the natural components, and then there is also the intent. Intention, at its core, is what you want to occur. Yet, it is more than wishful thinking and hope. Intention is at the base of any spell or rite that the practitioner decides to invoke.

Intention has become a topic that is frequently discussed by magickal practitioners and authors and is not a subject that comes without controversy. Though there is a lot of debate given to what intention is and how to use it, intention, in and of itself, is important to the production of a well-crafted spell. Without intention, you would simply have an idea for what was going to happen, but nothing specific to help guide what is about to happen.

Intention sets the tone for your magickal working or rite. A true intention is a thoughtform that has been seriously contemplated prior to magick being wrought. The thoughtform continues to work in the astral plane as you work in the physical plane. It provides the foundation for what one plans to do. It truly sets the resolve to see the act to completion. If you have a strong intention, it will pave the way for a strong spell.

Intention versus Will

What is the difference between intention and will? Intention is the change that one desires to bring about. While I may have decided to work with a spell that centers around healing, my intention is what will shape the spell. It is the impact that I want to make. This could range from wanting to heal the earth of the harmful pollutants put out by factories to striving to impact the effect of cancer on a close friend. The two ways that I approach the concept of healing are completely dependent upon my intention.

When intent is paired with other foundational practices of the Craft, you have direction for your spell.

When I began studying the Craft, I was introduced to the Witch's Pyramid. There are four tenets that accompany the Witch's Pyramid: to know, to dare, to will, and to remain silent. Intention affects each of these concepts, which in turn affect the spell itself.

A LITTLE BIT OF MAGIC

In order for the spell to be successful, you need to make sure that you carefully craft your intent—be specific, polite, proactive, synergistic, and repetitious.

To Know: This aspect of the Witch's Pyramid is in direct correlation with intention. We must know what we are working for. We must know what components correspond to our intention in order to see it to fruition. We need to know how to interlace all of them together to make it work.

To Dare: This corner of the Witch's Pyramid requires that we be willing to act on our intentions. This is where we focus on our intent to create a new reality.

To Will: This is quite possibly the most important aspect of the Witch's Pyramid, and it works in conjunction with intent. We may know what we need to do. Will puts our knowledge into action. Here we take our idea, our concept, and utilize our tools and correspondences to produce a tangible result.

To Be Silent: This concept refers to whether we are able to carry our intention into actuality. Our culture is one of instant gratification, and it can be difficult to keep to ourselves what we have done as we desire recognition. However, by consistently placing our own positive energy into our intent, we block out negativity that could derail our spellwork.

Setting Your Intention

It is important when putting together a spell that you set your intention. What I mean by this is that you need to be able to define what type of spell you are doing along with how you will execute it to try to achieve your desired result. Most importantly, you need to be able to articulate why you are doing it. Be specific! The more you focus on what you are doing, the better your result will be.

There are several ways that you can set your intention. It often helps that you state what it is, either in writing or verbally. This can make the idea become more concrete. It gives the thoughts form and substance that can then be molded into a spell or ritual that can be conducted by the individual or group.

I like to create visual charts that help me visualize what I am working for. On the next page is an example of a chart that I might complete when outlining a spell. I have provided some examples of types

Type of Spell	Intentions	Timing	Tools	Color	Stone	Plant/Oil
Communication	To increase positive communication between myself and other parties	Wednesday, sunrise or noon, waxing Moon	Book of Shadows, wand	Orange, yellow	Carnelian, amber, citrine	Lavender, jasmine
Courage	To overcome fear of heights	Tuesday, sunrise or noon, waxing or Full Moon	Athame, sword	Red or orange	Garnet, ruby	Dragon's blood
Divination	To increase my abilities with tarot	Monday, midnight, dark of the Moon	Tarot cards, cauldron	Silver or white	Moonstone, opal	Honeysuckle, moonflower
Health	To increase the skeletal healing in my son, who has a break in his arm	Sunday, noon Full Moon	Boline, thurible or censer	Yellow, orange	Sunstone, amber	Lemon, citrus, sunflowers
Love	To attract romantic love into my life	Friday, evening or twilight, waxing Moon	Besom, chalice	Pink, red, or copper	Rose quartz, jade	Iris, lilac, vanilla
Prosperity	To increase my ability to provide for my family	Thursday, sunrise, waxing Moon	Pentacle, besom	Black, silver	Jet, obsidian, hematite	Mint, patchouli
Protection	To provide protection for our new property and home	Saturday, twilight or midnight, New Moon	Athame, bell	Purple, indigo, blue	Amethyst, charoite, turquoise	Belladonna, patchouli

of spells that I might work with. When I prepare a spell, I have the timing of the spell listed out for reference. I also write out what types of tools I might work with and any other items I could possibly want to include. Then I fill out the chart with my intentions clearly listed. The table to the left is by no means an exhaustive listing of correspondences, but it includes ones that have worked for me over time.

When Your Spell Goes Awry

Unfortunately, sometimes not even the best-planned or best-executed spells work the way we envision. Either the spell seems not to work at all or the result is totally not what we expected. So, what does it mean when an occurrence like this happens?

Missing the Big Picture

Human beings have a knack for thinking we know best. While we do often have an idea of what we think is in our own best interests, there are times when we neglect to see the larger picture. There are times when it seems like we are wearing blinders and can only see things that are directly in front of us, or in the case of spell work, we only see what we want to see that is in conjunction with our spell.

When we are doing work in our coven, for instance, we will often put in a tagline: "if it is in the interest of my higher self." This allows us to work in time with universal energies that may be at play. It also gives us a chance to be a bit humble in that we may not always know what is best for us.

Working Out for the Best

There have also been times when a spell just flat out does not work how we envisioned that it would. Either the outcome ends up being different from what we asked for or it simply does not work. Both options have occurred for me and both are completely okay. There is always a reason why things have worked out as they have.

I usually write down all my spells and keep them until I have an outcome. If the outcome differed from what I intended or expected, then I try to sort out why. I analyze what my intent was and look

at the outcome. What happened? Did it work to any extent? If so, then I take a closer look at the wording that I used in my spell. There have been times when I have come back to the spell several years down the line. It may have worked—just not on the timeline I would have liked. There are also times that things have not worked at all and it was in my best interests, as what I was working for may not have been reasonable.

• • • ☽ • • •

In life, there are many paths that lie in front of us. Crafting spells and rites is no different. We attempt to channel and direct the spells into what we feel would be the best outcome. Intention itself will not make a successful spell. You have to have all the components working together in harmony to give yourself the best opportunity and trust that the gods and goddesses know what is best when things do not go according to plan. However, when a strong intention is matched with equally strong magickal foundations, you set yourself up for success.

Magickal Influences and Principles of Hermeticism

Raven Digitalis

A word that frequents occult, historical, and scholarly texts of all varieties is *Hermeticism.* The word is derived from the name of the Greek-Egyptian mythic figure *Hermes Trismegistus,* meaning "thrice-great Hermes," and refers to the spiritual and religious movement that occurred after the Greek conquest of Egypt by Alexander the Great in 332 BCE. Alexander's death shortly thereafter (323 BCE) began what is known as the Hellenistic Period, in which old worldviews were threatened by cultural merging. The centuries of transition between Alexander's conquests and the beginning of the Common Era marked the rise of a pagan variant of Gnosticism now termed Hermeticism.

Because readers of this almanac come from a wide variety of occult and spiritual backgrounds, this article is meant for readers of all types to learn and practice with success. I will explore the magick and history of the Hermetic movement, and we will then integrate practical esoteric exercises that can be put right into practice in daily life.

In short, the Hermetic movement was a culturally blended response to the syncretism of spiritual systems of the time, namely the ancient Greco-Roman and Egyptian religious systems. Philosophies, cosmologies, and magickal practices from these systems and others mixed and mingled, eventually creating a distinct current of thought and practice. Hermeticism is not a "religion" by common definition, but is better described as philosophical and spiritual movement. The "three parts of the philosophy of the whole world," which the Emerald Tablet of Hermes Trismegistus mentions, are alchemy, astrology, and theurgy, all of which were cornerstones of blended Hermetic teachings.

It's impossible to study the expansion of magick and mysticism in the Western world without some understanding of Hermeticism. That's why magicians, Witches, Pagans, and occultists like ourselves can greatly benefit from knowing a bit of the history. After all, it's part of our own spiritual lineage!

Hermetic material encompasses astrology, astronomy, alchemy, spellcraft, mystical philosophy, natural magick, planetary magick, elemental magick, and the metaphysical correspondences of herbs, incenses, gemstones, days of the week, animals, and body parts. Numerous religious and occult movements grew, and continue to grow from, Hermetic soil, and virtually all magickal paths have been influenced to some degree by Hermeticism.

A LITTLE BIT OF MAGIC

By understanding the place of magic in ancient times, as well as cross-culturally, our personal practices can become enriched with new and inspiring perspectives.

The Hermetic Order of the Golden Dawn was founded in 1888. The development of what are called *Western Mystery Traditions* was overwhelmingly Hermetic in nature. Hermeticism influenced the likes of Wicca, Thelema, Freemasonry, and countless other modern spiritual paths and offshoots.

It can easily be said that Hermeticism is the most unified, encompassing, and influential spiritual movement sprouting from Western antiquity!

Modern traditions of Witchcraft are known to have been influenced by the Golden Dawn and its various Hermetic aspects. Even Gerald Gardner himself, the cocreator of modern Wicca, once hinted at the likelihood that a number of traditional Wiccan rituals were, at least in part, created or influenced by members of the Golden Dawn as well as earlier fraternal lodge traditions, including Freemasonry.

Wicca and other traditions of Witchcraft make use of casting a circle: a sacred space between the worlds. Witches also invoke elemental watchtowers, often using invoking pentagrams to do so. These aspects, as well as a number of sacred tools or "weapons," as they're called in some traditions, were borrowed or adapted from Golden Dawn material, upon which earlier Hermetic schools had profound esoteric influence. This is our legacy.

Hermetic Threads

The Cosmic Egg

There are a number of curious crossovers and similarities between ancient Egyptian culture, Greco-Roman culture, and even traditional Jewish Kabbalah. For starters, the symbolism of the Cosmic Egg is also present in Greek mythology as the Orphic Egg. The Greek legend is that the whole of the universe was birthed from a silver egg. This egg is often depicted with a serpent perfectly coiled around it. Because of Egypt's vast influence on the Western world, it's quite possible that the Greeks adopted this imagery from the Egyptian tale of creation.

If the yolk of the Cosmic Egg is all Positive (manifest) Existence, its albumen, or white, is comparable to the Realms of Negative Existence in the Kabbalistic view. The Kabbalistic description of Ein Soph comes from the *Sepher Yetzirah* text. The realm of Ein Soph exists above the Tree of Life and is said to be the Great Nothingness from which the Tree of Life (and thus all of existence) was born. Ein Soph is sometimes broken into three distinct Veils of Negative Existence—these are included in studies within the Hermetic Order

of the Golden Dawn as Ein, Ein Soph, and Ein Soph Aur. In traditional Kabbalism, Ein Soph is *nihil*; that is, it has no associations beyond it being the inaccessible primordial nothingness from which all came about.

Put it into practice: Find a cozy nook in nature that you can meditate in. Ideally, this location should allow you to be "tucked away" out of view from others where you can be intimately surrounded by the beauty of Mother Nature. Bring an egg with you; ensure that the egg is cruelty-free, meaning that it should either be procured from a local farmer or free range. Sit in the nook with the egg in your lap and take a series of deep breaths. Visualize the egg expanding until it surrounds your body with a silver-colored shell of protection. As you inhale, visualize yourself taking in the essence of the nourishing yolk. Feel the nourishing and protective essence of nature and the cosmos entering your body, mind, and spirit. When you feel a sense of completion, thank the gods and the universe in your own words, finishing by kissing the egg and leaving it in nature.

The Tarot

Many occultists believe the tarot to have made its way to Europe from India by way of Egypt. The scholarly consensus is that the tarot was created in Italy in the early fifteenth century by Marziano da Tortona, secretary to Filippo Maria Visconti (the Duke of Milan). However, a possible early Egyptian prototype for the cards, or at least some of their concepts, has been suggested. If the tarot indeed has its origins in ancient Egypt, would it be appropriate to suggest that various conceptions of the Kabbalistic Tree also have origins in early Egyptian and Hermetic traditions?

The standard tarot cards align perfectly with the Kabbalistic Tree of Life. The twenty-two major arcana each have an association with a path on the tree (of which there are twenty-two), and the ten number cards align with the ten Sephiroth, or Fruits of the Tree (these are considered emanations of God). There are four suits to the tarot, giving each Sephirah four cards, which correspond to the Kabbalistic notion of the Four Worlds that make up the Tree of Life. Here are the names of these levels of existence and some alignments according to the Golden Dawn:

Atziluth: The Archetypal World; *Yod,* wands, Sephirah 1 (Kether)
Briah: The Creative World; *Heh,* cups, Sephiroth 2 and 3
Yetzirah: The World of Formation; *Vau,* swords, Sephiroth 4 to 9
Assiah: The Material World; *Heh,* pentacles, Sephirah 10 (Malkuth)

Put it into practice: Take your favorite pack of tarot or oracle cards and separate the deck by numbers. For example, place all the tens together, all the nines together, and so on. Place the major arcana in a separate numerically ordered stack. With a pen and notepad in hand, light a candle and incense, and get comfy. Meditate on each stack of cards beginning with the aces. Regardless of your own Kabbalistic or tarot knowledge, take notes on what each stack means to you. What are the symbolic and energetic similarities you see or feel between the cards of each stack? Which symbolism stands out to you the most? How do these cards make you feel spiritually? Feel free to do the same with each subsequent major arcana card if you feel called to do so. Use the notes you've taken to help deepen your own tarot discoveries throughout your personal esoteric path.

The Caduceus

Both Hermes and Hermes Trismegistus are depicted as holding the caduceus wand. The caduceus is a symbol that was utilized in classical Greco-Roman civilization. It is depicted as a wand with a Ketheric light and wings at its top, and two snakes are perfectly coiled around the rod. The snake imagery can be compared to the Vedic concept of the *kundalini*, a force of the human energy system symbolized as serpents ascending around the spine from the base chakra to the (again Ketheric) crown chakra; the esoteric teachings of kundalini are most prevalent in Shakta (Goddess-centric) Tantric schools of Hinduism.

Some early versions of the Kabbalistic Tree depict the tree within an oval, further demonstrating the Cosmic Egg concept. The snake coiled around the Orphic Egg in the Greek view is analogous to the Path of the Serpent. Many Kabbalistic magicians align to the energetic current of the caduceus through the Path of the Serpent, which entails, in a process of theurgic magic, the opening of each Sephirah on the Tree of Life, beginning with Malkuth and ending with Kether.

It's also interesting to note that the serpent has been viewed as a phallic symbol for eons across Pagan traditions, and in modern terms, represents the spiral coiling of DNA. Is this simply cosmic synchronicity, or did the ancients possess a bit more wisdom than they're usually accredited?

In the Torah/Bible's Book of Numbers, God (Yahweh) instructs Moses to craft a bronze serpent (the Nehustan) affixed to a pole to cure snake-bitten Israelites of their venomous wounds. In Jewish and Kabbalistic terms, the serpent is also aligned to the story of the snake of temptation in the Garden of Eden. I would venture to guess that elements of these scriptural tales were borrowed from Egyptian symbolism, or perhaps even vice versa. Idea and symbolism were so widely shared during the rise of Hermeticism that both possibilities are valid options.

Put it into practice: Something termed the *frequency illusion* (or the *Baader-Meinhof phenomenon*) affirms that when we expect or aim to see something, we will see it. For example, if we are constantly thinking about the deer as a spirit animal, we are likely to see deer everywhere, whether in media, writing, or everyday life. Try this with the caduceus: for the next week, look for this symbol when you're walking, driving, watching television, and so on. Every time you see the symbol, bring to mind its symbolism as an ancient metaphysical symbol of healing and enlightenment. Tap into its global astral imprint by taking a deep breath while you look at the symbol, envisioning its timeless healing light entering your body and strengthening your holistic wellness.

The Seven Principles of Hermeticism

I find that the seven principles of Hermeticism, as recognized in modern Hermetic thought, are of particular importance to the spiritual practitioner because of their emphasis on the mind-body-spirit connection.

Published in 1912 by Paul Foster Case, Michael Witty, and William Walker Atkinson (Yogi Ramacharaka) under the collective pseudonym the Three Initiates, an occult text called *The Kybalion* has gained the reputation as a significant book on modern Hermetic commentary. The text, which is short but profound, sheds a concise light on seven select principles of ancient Hermetic thought. Readers familiar with modern Witchcraft and other magickal systems are likely to recognize esoteric crossovers within their own philosophical framework. The principles discussed, which I feel are particularly relevant for magickal souls and anyone following an emotionally driven spiritual system, are as follows:

The Principle of Mentalism

All things in existence and physical reality spring forth from the mental plane. The mind of humankind is a reflection of the Infinite Mind and is the source of all perceptive and psychic power. The only substantial thing in reality is the mind, from which everything in reality derives.

Put it into practice: This principle is similar to the Law of Attraction, which has grown in the forefront of popular New Age culture. As an ancient principle, it's been long understood that we humans cocreate our own realities. Reflect back on your week while you think about how your experience seemed to match your mental state throughout. As time moves onward, try actively shifting your state of mind to see how much your own experience changes as a result. This existential exercise takes a lot of patience and a lot of practice, but it can truly help us understand the power of thought.

The Principle of Correspondence

"As above, so below; as below, so above": existence is upheld through corresponding forces, being the origin of spiritual paradox. The principles of one thing correspond to the principles of another thing; reality functions as a mirror.

Put it into practice: Hop onto YouTube and watch some videos about the cosmos. Have a good time studying the universe, allowing it to instill that humble sense of wonder we so often feel as children. Later, research videos about atoms and quantum mechanics. Consider how the Great Above corresponds to the Great Below; the uncanny realizations might surprise you!

The Principle of Vibration

Nothing in reality is physically unchanging; everything is a vibration or pattern of energy. Because nothing is static or fixed, the only constant is change. Everything is a manifestation of the All or the Great Mind, and vibration is the reason that anything can exist as its "own" distinct thing (a book, a river, a thought, etc.) instead of remaining one.

Put it into practice: Find an old chipped cup, plate, or vase that you no longer use. Using a permanent marker or paint, take the item and draw some of the magickal symbols mentioned in this article. When ready, go somewhere that you can drop the object, allowing it to shatter. Once it's shattered, perform an act of divination by looking at the pieces to see if they form any symbols that are psychologically significant to you personally. Additionally, reflect on the reality of change as the only constant in reality.

The Principle of Polarity

Reality is duality. Like the Taoist principle of yin and yang, this asserts that everything has its equal opposite yet is part of the same unity. Because all of existence is polarized, both thesis and antithesis (one thing and its complete opposite) are simultaneously true and untrue—a global paradox that obliterates notions of absolutes in any area of life.

Put it into practice: Inquire with a local school or college about public debates you may be able to attend. Otherwise, look up some debates online to which you personally may feel a neutral emotional response. Whether the debate is academic, political, social, or spiritual, try to empathize with each party's contrasting viewpoints. Is it possible that each party can be both right and wrong simultaneously?

The Principle of Rhythm
Action and reaction, the life cycle of birth and eventual death, the ascent and descent of a sea's tide . . . These occurrences account for this principle, which affirms that nothing ever exists as one of its polarities but is ever fluctuating. Knowing this, a person can consciously choose to not fall to one extreme or another in any area of life.

Put it into practice: Test the elements. As conscious souls incarnated in a human frame, we are at the mercy of the elements around us. We must always strike a balance in order to maintain footing in life. Think about what it would feel like to run your finger quickly through a candle flame in order to find your threshold for a small amount of pain. Think about the ways we humans harness fire and electricity to better our lives, and how we must maintain a balance before it becomes a force that can overtake us. Get creative by experimenting with your thresholds surrounding the elements air, water, and earth—just be cautious!

The Principle of Cause and Effect

Nothing is happenstance; everything is a result of something else. One can either choose to act as a social chess piece for others' whims, desires, norms, and conditionings, or one can choose to both individualize and take power over their own bodies, thoughts, actions, emotions, and experiences.

Put it into practice: Situate yourself comfortably in a sacred space or somewhere that feels calming to you—perhaps the bathtub! Think about different times in your life where you may have "deposited" energy and could still be linked by an astral cord that cuts through time and space. These cords can be draining. Using whichever magickal tools toward which you feel drawn, sever any unhealthy energetic cords from your body. Envision them returning to their own space-time with a big blast of light, and fill your body with this cosmic light as you work on each connection. Remember to go easy on yourself and that healing is a lifelong path.

The Principle of Gender

Everything in reality is an amalgam of the feminine and the masculine. Both forces exist within each other, and neither force exists independently or as an absolute. Everything and everyone is a combination of masculine and feminine energies rather than being one or the other, and its manifestation on the physical plane is one's biological sex, which can be male, female, or in between.

Put it into practice: Do some research into atypical gender expressions, including identities such as transgender, gender fluid, genderqueer, nonbinary, third gendered, and nongendered. Explore how different cultures throughout time have observed noncisgendered folks, in both ancient and modern times. Research and reflect upon the difference between sex (biological) and gender (social/spiritual). You may even feel inclined to turn it up a notch by doing some cross-dressing (also called drag or transvestitism) in order to see how it affects you psychologically and spiritually—after all, a little gender-bending never hurt anyone!

Resources

D'Este, Sorita, and David Rankine. *Wicca Magickal Beginnings: A Study of the Possible Origins of the Rituals and Practices Found in This Modern Tradition of Pagan Witchcraft and Magick*. London: Avalonia Press, 2008.

Doreal, trans. *The Emerald Tablets of Thoth-the-Atlantean*. Nashville, TN: Source Books, 2002.

Fowden, Garth. *The Egyptian Hermes: A Historical Approach to the Late Pagan Mind*. Princeton, NJ: Princeton University Press, 1993.

Greer, John Michael. *The New Encyclopedia of the Occult*. St. Paul, MN: Llewellyn Pulications, 2003.

Harris, Stephen L., and Gloria Platzner. *Classical Mythology: Images & Insights*. Mountain View, CA: Mayfield Publishing, 1995.

Kinney, Jay, ed. *The Inner West: An Introduction to the Hidden Wisdom of the West*. New York: Tarcher/Penguin, 2004.

McNevin, Estha. Opus Aima Obscuræ tradition materials and lesson notes. Missoula, MT, 2018.

Salaman, Clement, Dorine Van Oven, William D. Wharton, Jean-Pierre Mahé. *The Way of Hermes: New Translations of the Corpus Hermeticum and the Definitions of Hermes Trismegistus to Asclepius*. Rochester, VT: Inner Traditions, 2002.

Three Initiates. *The Kybalion*. New York: Tarcher/Penguin, 2008.

Wildoak, Peregrin. "The Influence of the Golden Dawn on Modern Wicca." Scribd. PDF. Accessed August 2018. https://www.scribd.com /document/113929296/The-Influence-of-the-Golden-Dawn-on-the -Magic-of-Wicca.

Zalewski, Pat. *Kabbalah of the Golden Dawn*. Edison, NJ: Castle Books, 2000.

Creating a Magical Bindrune

Kate Freuler

If you've ever read fiction about sorcery or watched movies about Vikings, chances are you've stumbled across runes. It may surprise some people to know that these mysterious glyphs aren't just cinematic decoration. Runes are ancient primitive symbols that make up an alphabet originating in Northern Europe in the second century. They were first used by long-gone Teutonic tribes and have survived all the way into the present. Runes are most popularly utilized nowadays as a divination tool and as a code-like way of writing.

The ongoing popularity of the runes is truly amazing. Runic inscriptions dating back as far as 150 CE have been found, and they've been putting in appearances throughout history ever since. They've been used by armies during war, engraved into weapons and shields, and carved into objects for magical and religious purposes. Like many symbols, over time their meanings have been twisted around by different people to fit their needs, and of course this includes a dark side. Runes themselves are not, and were never meant to be, hate symbols, but I recently learned that some of them have very sadly been appropriated by white supremacist groups. On the other side of the spectrum, runes also appear in Disney movies, junior fiction, and in the logos of popular companies. Take a look at the logo for Bluetooth—it's actually the initials of a tenth-century king of Denmark written in runes! Runes are so old that they have seen the good, the bad, and the ugly of humankind. To me, this makes them incredibly powerful tools for use in magic.

What Are Runes, Exactly?

Runes are twenty-four symbols that make up the old Teutonic alphabet. Different types of runes can be found on historic memorials and artifacts. There are several different versions of the runic alphabet, but here we will be discussing the oldest Germanic one, called the Elder Futhark: "Elder" because it is the oldest and "Futhark" because that is the modern linguistic interpretation of the first seven letters of the runic alphabet. While for the most part runes correspond with the letters of the modern English alphabet and they're used for writing words sometimes, originally they were used as symbols in and of themselves. Much of runic knowledge was passed down verbally and so the meanings have flowed and evolved over time. Even the word *rune* itself, rooted in old Germanic and Nordic languages, translates to mean "mystery" or "secret."

Each rune is said to represent an object, circumstance, or force. This makes them excellent tools for divination; you can purchase a multitude of rune sets, engraved in wood, rock, clay, and even crystals. Rune divination can fill a whole book on its own, so in this article we will be discussing how to use runes for magic, specifically by creating what are known as *bindrunes*. A bindrune is simply grouping several runes together to join forces to meet a specific end, sort of like putting together an emblem that encapsulates your magical objective. It combines deeply symbolic images, magical intent and a little artistry.

I created a bindrune for myself years ago that I had tattooed on my stomach to represent fertility, blessings, and protection. Later it became the logo for my online Witchcraft shop. I have to say it has worked out to be fortuitous and positive, like I intended both personally and professionally. This simple symbol, drawn over and over again so many times in my daily life and work, has become powerful and meaningful to me in a deeply ingrained way. Maybe you too will create a personal power symbol from the runes that lasts your whole life.

Understanding the Elder Futhark

To effectively create a magical bindrune, you must first comprehend the meaning of each distinct symbol. Once you understand them individually, innumerable ways for you to work magic with runes will appear. The following is a list of the Elder Futhark runes and their meanings:

Rune	Name	Letter	Meaning
ᚠ	Fehu	F	Prosperity. Fulfillment. Earned income one has worked hard for. An increase in wealth. Successful financial investments. A conquest. Money that is earned, not won. Stability and nourishment. A rune of employment and security.
ᚢ	Uruz	U	Strength. Proving oneself in work, business, or life. Added responsibility. Rite of passage. Coming of age. Willpower. Determination. Stamina. Success through hard work. Promotion. Outgrowing the old and welcoming the new. A big change requiring warrior strength and falling on one's own resources.
ᚦ	Thurisaz	Th	Help and protection. A warning to others. This rune translates roughly to "thorn," which plants use to protect themselves and ward off predators.
ᚨ	Ansuz	A	Messenger rune. Spoken words. Communication. Receiving signals. Honest advice. Knowledge and wisdom bestowed by a teacher. Apprenticeship. This rune is especially associated with education, examinations, or intellectual tests of all kinds.
ᚱ	Raido	R	Travel. Vacation. A safe and pleasant journey. News from afar. Strategic action.
ᚲ	Kano	K	Fire. Opening. Breaking through the darkness and finding understanding. Health. Positivity. Energy. Recovery. Confidence. New relationships. Creativity.
ᚷ	Gebo	G	A gift. Partnership. Love. Friendship. Relationships. Mutual support. Generosity. Harmony. This is a rune associated with love. In modern times, you can see this rune when we sign a letter with *XOXO;* the X means a kiss.
ᚹ	Wunjo	W	Joy and light. Happiness. Fulfillment in love or career. Good fortune, positive outcomes, joy in one's work, especially for craftspeople and artists. Good news and successful travels.
ᚺ	Hagalaz	H	Natural disaster. Unavoidable destruction that is natural and for the best. Events beyond your control. Natural limitations that must be accepted. Life-changing events. Chance.

Rune	Name	Letter	Meaning
ᚾ	Nauthiz	N	Need. Necessity. Constraint. Pain. Limitations. Slowness. Oppression. Lack. Common sense. Practicality. Prudence. A problem that can only be fixed by patience and the passage of time. A long-standing issue or illness. This rune can be utilized to aid in acceptance of one's limitations, as well as induce patience and self-restraint.
ᛁ	Isa	I	Ice. Standstill. Frozen. Plans being put on hold. A dark time. Isolation. A cooling off of passions. Separation. In making a bindrune, Isa can be used to "freeze" or preserve a situation as it is.
ᛃ	Jera	J	Harvest. Positive outcomes. Tangible results and recognition after hard work. Reward after a period of patience. Long-term goals reached. Jera is also the rune of justice and legal matters, contracts and bureaucracy. Sometimes this rune is interpreted to mean "one year" or one turning of the Wheel of the Year.
ᛇ	Eihwaz	Y	Defense against danger. Aversion. Minor catastrophe that is in the end for your own good. A necessary setback. This rune can be used to transform obstacles into opportunities.
ᛈ	Perth	P	Secrets coming into the light. Initiation. Finding lost things. Something hidden being discovered. Occult powers. Divination.
ᛉ	Algiz	Z	Positive new influence in life. Protection. A willing sacrifice of something lesser for something greater. Algiz acts a shield against all harm and negative influences and is best known as a protection rune.
ᛋ	Sowelu	S	The sun. Wholeness. Clear thinking. Success in all undertakings. Achievement. Victory. Health. Strength. Energy.
ᛏ	Teiwaz	T	Warrior energy. Victory in battle. Courage. Competition. Will. Motivation. Fighting for what is right. Activism.
ᛒ	Berkana	B	Growth. Rebirth. Flowing into new form. Family and babies. Spouse, home, and children. Fertility. Birth of a child or an idea. Mother and child. Family celebration. Berkana is a rune of nurturing, which can be applied to a new life or bringing any project or idea into physical being.

Rune	Name	Letter	Meaning
ᛖ	Ehwaz	Eo	Transition. Travel. Planned change for the better. Journey. Progress. Movement. A physical change of location.
ᛗ	Mannaz	M	Humankind. Interdependence. Cooperation. Giving and receiving assistance from others. Help and sound advice. The relationship with the self. Group activities. Collaboration. Goodwill between people.
ᛚ	Laguz	L	Water. Flow. Unseen powers. Emotions. Awakening the intuition. Deep knowing. The moon. Spirituality. Psychic ability.
◇	Inguz	Ng	Completion. New life path. Resolution of the old to start something new. Successful conclusion of projects and plans. Freedom from worry. Fertility or birth of a new stage in life. When creating a bindrune, Inguz can be used to keep other runes together, to hold them in place and prevent their energy being drained away.
ᛞ	Dagaz	D	New resolutions. Growth. Measured progress. Change in attitude. Positive outlook. Seeing the bright side. Breakthrough. Achievement and prosperity.
ᛟ	Othila	O	Material things. Land. House. Property. Inherited possessions. Legacy. Heirlooms. Protection of property. This rune can also represent inherited personality traits and genetic qualities.
	Wyrd		The blank rune. No letter—the unknowable. Fate. Karma. That which is predestined and cannot be changed. The blank rune is the source of much argument among rune enthusiasts. Some say that the original Elder Futhark didn't have a blank rune and therefore disregard it as a New Age invention. Others choose to include the blank rune in their readings and work. Since it is not in fact any physical symbol, we won't be able to use it in a bindrune; however, I've included it here for the sake of knowledge.

Making Your Own Bindrune

Now that you know the meanings of each rune, you can layer several of them together to make one symbol, aimed toward a specific end.

Traditionally, bindrunes contain an uneven number of three, five, or seven runes. Add more than that, and the symbol can become unwieldy. As you can see, the runes are quite simple shapes and are often hidden within each other. For example, Wunjo ᛈ is also visible in the Thurisaz rune ᚦ, and Ehwaz ᛗ is visible in the Mannaz ᛘ rune. However it's important to note that these runes have very different meanings, and accidentally mixing them up together will negate the one that is less visible. For this reason, it's important to make sure each symbol within the bindrune maintains its own status and is not overridden by another rune. You do not want Isa | to disappear into Teiwaz ↑, for then Isa would lose its meaning. In other words, all runes in a bindrune must be drawn independently and stand on their own. The only exception to this is when two runes share a center staff and both extend off of it. If I blend Teiwaz ↑ and Fehu ᚠ, they could be written like this: ↑ᚠ. Both are still easily recognizable and equally present.

To create your own bindrune, select several runes according to their meaning and your goal. Get a pencil and paper and draw them overlapping in different ways, experimenting to see what you come up with. The symbol you create has to resonate with you. When it looks and feels right, you will know. See the following examples to get inspired. As you learn about the runes and their meanings, you will discover all kinds of aesthetically pleasing and useful combinations to put to use in your everyday life.

I like to embellish my final bindrunes with dots to create a balanced look, and also because the dots have an anchoring feel to them. I also sometimes add swirls and other flourishes, whereas some people like the plain, blunt look of the original symbols. This is something for you to play around with and decide for yourself.

Bindrune for Academics

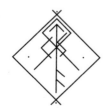

This is a bindrune to attract success in scholarly pursuits or help with passing exams. Ansuz ᚨ represents education, Teiwaz ↑ means victory, and Sowelu ᛋ blesses your endeavors with successful Sun power. Kano ᚲ opens the way to the new opportunities that are available upon succeeding at your lessons. Holding these all together is Inguz ◇, which means completion.

Bindrune for Family Protection

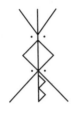

To make a bindrune for protection, try Algiz Y, which signifies protection from all harm and negativity regarding the issue. Add runes to its center staff reflecting what you wish to protect, in this case home and family. For this goal, use Berkana ß for family and Othila ⨯ for house and property. You can use different runes with Algiz depending on what you wish to protect.

Bindrune for Prosperity

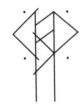

To create a bindrune for attracting prosperity, draw Fehu Ϝ in the center to represent material stability, Wunjo ϼ for financial success, and Jera ⟨⟩ to signify harvesting rewards.

Bindrune for Friendship

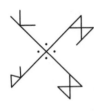

To surround yourself with good people and friendships, use Gebo X to attract fortuitous relationships, and on the spokes of this rune, add Kano ⟨ for positive new beginnings, Raido ᚱ for happy journeys and experiences, Mannaz ᛗ for teamwork and goodwill from others, and Dagaz ᛞ for positive attitudes.

Bindrune for Restraint

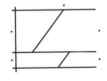

Not all the runes have happy connotations, but even the negative ones are useful when it comes to banishing or controlling qualities of ourselves we wish to lessen. Here is a bindrune for self-restraint that can be worn to curb unhealthy habits. Nauthiz ᛏ is for holding back unhealthy urges or cravings, Hagalaz ᚺ acts as recognition that a habit is out of your control, and Isa | to "freeze" it, or put a stop to it. In this case Isa | is placed along the side of the other runes, touching both and freezing them still. For aesthetics, this bindrune includes two of the runes on their sides, which shows how artistry can play a role in your final design. When I drew this bindrune upright, I didn't like the aesthetic, which affected how I felt about it. When I flipped it on its side, I liked how it looked, and this made it easier for me to connect with it. Aesthetics do matter; you have to like the symbol you create for it to resonate with you.

Charging Your Bindrune

Once you've decided on your final design, you must empower your bindrune. Draw it on paper and place it on your altar. Cast a circle if you wish, and call upon your chosen deities if you have them.

For the sake of explanation, I'm going to use the family protection rune as an example here.

First, imagine each rune separately and what they represent to you. Focus on Algiz Y, which is like a shield. Imagine a bubble of white protective light around your home life. Then, contemplate Othila ⋈ and visualize your house, vehicle, and important possessions. Look at Berkana ᛒ and imagine your loved ones. This creates a mental link to each rune separately, giving them a "job" so to speak. Then, look at the bindrune as a whole and see it pulsing with protective, loving energy. Using your finger, draw a circle around the symbol. Feel the vibration going from your hands into the bindrune. Now the bindrune is ready to be used.

Ways to Use Your Bindrune

- Draw it on paper and use it in spells by burning it, burying it, or simply keeping in your pocket.
- Draw your bindrune somewhere on your body with marker or henna where it cannot be seen, to draw upon its energy.
- Make it into a piece of jewelry by carving it in wood or clay.
- Trace it with your finger upon objects you wish to imbue with its energy.
- Paint it on a pebble or coin and keep it with you.
- Carve your symbol into a large piece of clay and hang on the wall, or paint it on canvas and display it.
- Etch your bindrune in the dirt of your yard to attract or repel.
- Draw protective runes in the air over doors and windows.

- If a bindrune is meant to impact another person, ask their permission to put it with their belongings or in their home.
- Make custom bindrunes for your magically inclined friends as gifts.

You can use your bindrune over and over again or create new ones as needed. I do both: sometimes I use the same symbol repeatedly, like my business logo/tattoo, because it has been fortuitous. Other times, depending on the working I'm doing, I make only one copy of the bindrune and then completely let go of the symbol after using it.

Now that you know the meanings of the Elder Futhark runes, don't be surprised if you notice them everywhere. They pop up in nature and in everyday life all the time, from cracks in the road to seemingly random marks on trees. Consider these messages in code from the universe.

Selected Resources

Willis, Tony. *The Runic Workbook: Understanding and Using the Power of Runes.* New York: Sterling Publishing, 1986.

Blum, Ralph. *The Book of Runes.* New York: St. Martin's Press, 1983.

Making Air Tangible: Getting Your Hands on the Air Elemental

JD Hortwort

Of all the elements in magick, sylphs may be the hardest to conceptualize. The sylph is the air elemental. It embodies all those qualities we associate with air: light, electric, wispy, intellect (genius, even), ether. All these words describe the sylph and they don't do us a bit of good. Say them over and over again and you still can't see the element of air.

When we imagine the element of fire, we have the candle flame or balefire to help us connect with that energy—hot, dry, volatile, consuming, and potentially destructive. The same is true of water and earth. This is not true of air.

If you can't conceptualize air, how are you supposed to work with it? You reach out to it in a "language" to which it can relate. You speak to it on the wind, seek its guidance in the language of flowers, and commune with it in the smoke from the incense.

Before We Begin: Basic Guidelines

You can't reach out to sylphs without understanding a few basic guidelines. First, sylphs aren't faeries. Faeries may be airy but they are not sylphs. Sylphs are the embodiment of air and all those qualities (plus many more) that I mentioned above. They may take human form but tend to be invisible. They are a force of nature that can be as gentle as a summer breeze or as violent as a late-season hurricane. They don't have a lot of patience and they won't help you find your keys. If you ask properly, however, they might lend you insight.

Depending on your tradition, by contrast, faeries are entities that can have a variety of supernatural powers. Some are friendly to humans, like brownies. Others, like goblins, take a dimmer view of humans.

If you are of the Celtic tradition, you might consider the Tuatha Dé Danann to be fairies. Former occupants of Ireland, they agreed to move to the underworld after battling the Sons of Mil. Once there, they became the Seelie and Unseelie—in modern terms, faeries of goodness and darkness.

But this is a bit of a tangent. The point is, you can work with faeries and you can work with sylphs, but don't expect a sylph to be able or willing to do what a faery might do.

Here's another bit of advice. Often when we think of the elemental of air, we think of one of the few obvious natural embodiments—the storm. The storm is the element of air at its most apparent. You might be tempted to do a working to harness a bit of that energy for your magick. In my personal experience, that is a bad idea.

Once, as a novice Witch, I thought I might try connecting with elemental air as a storm approached my home. As I stood in the middle of my garden, dark clouds began to roll in and the wind picked up. Shadows melted into an overcast, graying landscape. In the distance, I could hear thunder.

"I have time to do this," I thought to myself.

Standing at a crossing of rows of summer vegetables, I began my meditation on the element. With every gust of wind that swirled I felt closer and closer to pure air energy. The organic smell of dried leaves on the forest floor filled the atmosphere around me, first blending and then separating from the sweet aroma of the nearby roses.

With my arms outstretched, I felt as if I might be hoisted upward. My meditation deepened. I began to feel a surge of electricity dancing all around me. Literally, the hairs on my arms stood up. Then, the exhilarating electricity turned into a million pinpricks as if I were being bitten by fire ants.

A loud, although still distant, clap of thunder brought me back to earth. I quickly grounded myself and hurried inside. Had I tapped into the power of the element of air? Or was I a foolish little Witch just a hair's breadth from being electrocuted in a summer storm? I prefer to think it was the former, but I know enough about lightning to tell anyone that doing magick outside in a rising thunderstorm is not a good idea.

Reaching Out to Sylphs

Fortunately, there are several safe methods to ask for assistance from sylphs.

Make Chimes

A simple way to reach out is through a wind chime. Sylphs are thought to be especially drawn to music. The light, random tones of chimes can be especially alluring to these elementals.

You may have a wind chime already. You can certainly purchase one. The material doesn't really matter, although a chime that produces light tones might be preferable to one that belts out baritone or bass notes.

You can also create your own chime with three clay pots, five large beads, some paint, and a three-foot length of yarn. If you plan to hang your chime outside, purchase a durable textile suited to exposure to changing outdoor conditions.

Clay pots are available in all shapes and sizes. However, for our purposes, a moderate-sized chime can be constructed with a four-inch, a six-inch, and an eight-inch diameter pot. For clarity, diameter is measured across the opening or top of the pot, not the side.

Pick a long-term or enduring goal. Maybe you would like peace and serenity for your home. Maybe you would like to attract good people into your life. Whatever your goal, paint each pot with appropriate colors and symbols. For example, to bring peace into your life, you might like to paint one pot deep blue, the second light blue, and the third white. Add symbols that mean peace to you, whether they are personal interpretations, runes, or others you might find in a metaphysical book. You can also simply write your desire onto the pots.

Tie a knot in the end of the yarn and string a bead onto the yarn. Next, measure upward on the

A LITTLE BIT OF MAGIC

Trying to wrap your head around sylphs is like trying to define genius— you can't always describe it, but you know it when you are in the presence of it.

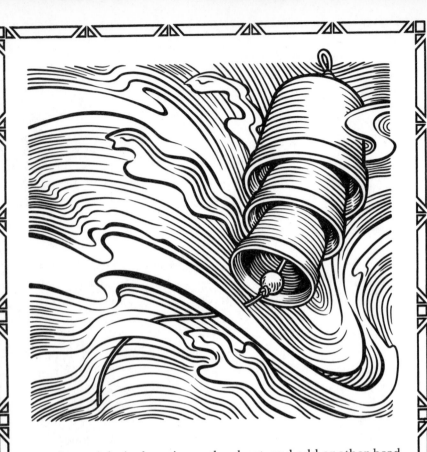

yarn about eight inches, tie another knot, and add another bead. Thread the four-inch pot onto the yarn using the center drain hole. Measure up the yarn another eight inches, tie another knot, add another bead and string the six-inch pot onto the assembly. Do the same with the final eight-inch pot. Each pot should "nest" slightly inside the other. You may need to adjust the placement of your knots to ensure the pots are nesting properly. This will make the sound when the chime is moved.

Add the last bead and tie a final knot at the top of the last pot. Use the remaining length of yarn to create a loop by which to hang the chime. Place the chime somewhere that you will walk past every day. Obviously, the main entrance to your home works, but if you live with others, the chime can be placed in your personal space.

Know that each time you ring the chime you are asking for assistance from the sylphs to bring your desire to fruition.

Flower Petal Insight

Because sylphs are believed to have access to all knowledge, they can be helpful in gaining insight into problems and situations. Another way to reach out to sylphs is with flower petals. Flowers are the parts of plants most associated with the element of air.

You can ask questions of the sylphs using a blend of petals and a large plate. I suggest using a handful each of red rose, calendula, lavender, and honeysuckle. All these flowers are associated with spirit or divination.

You will be casting these petals on a plate. I use a plain white plate. Just about any sort will do, but a simple colored plate is better than one with a pattern that might interfere with your reading. If you don't have a plate, you can draw a circle on a piece of paper.

Scrying with flower petals is not unlike scrying with tea leaves. You will be looking for patterns formed by the petals that you can interpret as they fall. Concentrate on the petals on the plate or inside the circle, not on the ones that fall off the plate or outside the circle.

In a place where you won't be disturbed, gather the flower petals in a bowl. If you like, light a floral incense stick. Place the plate on the table in front of you. If it helps, divide the plate in your mind between right and left hemispheres, labeling one "action" and the other one "no action." Or divide the plate into quarters and label each with an aspect of your life, such as family, career, finances, and disputes.

Close your eyes and stir the petals in the bowl. Contemplate your question. Focus on that question as you stir the petals.

When you are ready, keep your eyes closed, gather a handful of petals and let them fall on the plate as you make several circles above it. Use all the petals or stop when you feel it is right.

Open your eyes and review the results. You might find it helpful to get a resource on symbols for tea readings, especially if you are a novice. Don't expect the answer to jump off the plate immediately, although that can happen. For example, when I first experimented with this, I asked if scrying with flower petals was a good way to speak with air spirits. I got two clear and distinct "check marks" in the flowers.

This sort of scrying can take time to master. You may not get a clear answer at first. Write down your impressions and try again. You may find, after you've had time to mull it over, the answer suddenly smacks you right between the eyes!

You can keep your special blend of flower petals for future use. If you decide to dispose of them, take them to a nice natural setting and cast them to the wind in a respectful manner.

Scrying on Air

A final method of tapping into air energy is with smoke. The easiest way to get smoke is through incense. I'd like to say any incense will do, but I have reservations about that. For example, I love rosemary, but that is an invigorating scent. Peppermints and citrus odors are too. While that may not matter to the sylphs, these scents won't necessarily help you reach the meditative state necessary to receive messages from them.

Sage is a good choice, if you like that smell. Mugwort and rose are also good incenses to use. A classic blend used in European traditions is lavender and sandalwood.

To begin, prepare your space as you would your altar. You will need soft light. Candlelight is good, but make sure the flames won't distract you from the incense smoke. You may find it helpful to have a notebook and pen nearby to write down your reactions after your scrying session is complete.

Stick incense is the best to use. Most stick incenses will burn for ten to twenty minutes. That's plenty of time to make a connection. Remember, sylphs are notoriously impatient with humans. They aren't likely to hang around for an all-night marathon. Loose incense will provide smoke, but you have to constantly feed the charcoal with more herbs, and that can be disruptive to your meditation.

Light the incense. Get comfortable and arrange yourself so that you can see the smoke from the incense as it drifts up from the

stick. Begin by breathing deeply, eyes closed. Clear your mind from distractions. Even if you have a particular problem you want to ask about, I find the best mantra to focus on is a simple request:

Show me what I need to see.

When you are ready, open your eyes. This is the tricky part. You don't want to consciously "look" at the smoke. Your focus should be soft. Ideally, you aren't "looking" at anything. This leaves your mind open to everything. Be aware of the traces of white and gray wisps. See how they curl and sway. Like watching clouds overhead, perhaps you see a horse, then a boulder, then an eagle. Let the images flow.

Let the images come for as long as they will or until the incense burns out. Breathe deeply and let yourself become aware of your surroundings. How do you feel? Did you receive insight? Make notes about what you saw. Thank the spirits for helping you. If your answer came quickly, excellent! If you're not sure what you saw or what it means, sleep on it. Review your notes later and see if your answers become more apparent.

Finally

Working with sylphs can be challenging. Of all the elementals, they are the most standoffish. Don't assume that if you are an air sign astrologically speaking you'll have an easier time of it. I'm an air sign, and I've never found that sylphs come running any time I snap my fingers. In fact, snapping one's fingers at a sylph might be a definite way to ensure it doesn't respond!

But, if you are patient, if you have an open mind, and if you are willing to wait, you might find the sylph to be quite helpful—if a bit mercurial—as you learn to work with elementals.

Mythical Creatures, Real Animals

Lupa

An old song by Shel Silverstein talks about how Noah didn't take any unicorns on the ark because the creatures dallied so long that they were lost in the flood. Now, of course, Pagan mythologies are different, but it still comes down to the fact that we simply don't have physical unicorns here in this world and never have. But we do have other animals that in various ways resemble unicorns, dragons, mermaids, and other fantastic beasts.

You're certainly welcome to work with totems like Griffin or Phoenix, but they'll have a different, somewhat less grounded perspective on things. The totems of physical animals have more grounding in our world and more of an understanding of both what we need and what our planet needs. And because many of the animals who inspired the myths are now endangered, we can ask their totems what we can do to help them as a way of saying thank you for helping us.

Let's meet some of these worldly wonders!

Unicorns

Probably the most famous mythical being in the Western world, the unicorn is said to resemble a horse or deer with cloven hooves, a lion's tail, a goat's beard, and a single spiral horn in the center of its forehead. Neither deer nor horses have horns, of course; deer and antelope all have two horns, and horses never evolved to have any.

But the gemsbok, a type of African antelope, may look like it has only one straight, slender horn if viewed from the side, especially from a distance. The rings around the base look somewhat like spirals. And this large antelope does look a bit of a deer-horse hybrid with a lion-like tail. Take that, filter it through the flawed perception of the visiting Europeans who had seen nothing like it, add in a dash of the fantastic that was popular in Renaissance natural history writings, and voilà: unicorns! Of course, we had unicorn myths prior to this, but the gemsbok and other oryx species added fuel to the fantasy fire.

Another African creature with a claim for "real, live unicorn" is the rhinoceros. The white rhino has one horn, though close to the end of its nose rather than on its forehead. So do its eastern counterparts, the Indian and Javan rhinos. This hefty, armor-skinned animal is hardly the lithe, deerlike creature we think of as today's unicorn, but it's about the only animal with a single horn.

What of the narwhal, the unicorn of the sea? This sleek, fast whale does indeed have a single spiraling protrusion coming out of its forehead. This is no horn, but instead a modified tooth. The unicorn doesn't use it to fight, though. Instead, the tooth has lost

all its protective enamel, which makes it very sensitive. This allows the narwhal to use it to enhance the effectiveness of its echolocation. Narwhals will use the tusk to swat at cod to make them easier to catch, but they do so with relative gentleness so as to not injure the "horn."

Dragons

There are stories of dragons worldwide, though the most well-known come from Asia and Europe. Most often shown as great reptilian beings that may fly, breathe fire, bring good luck, and display other supernatural powers, dragons actually have a few down-to-earth sources.

Snakes are the most widespread of these. Found on every continent except Antarctica, their unusual legless ways of moving inspired many cultures to see them as amazing or fear-inducing creatures. And like a good fish story, the tales of these beasts grew larger and larger. Even when dragons have legs, many of them still retain serpentine traits.

Lizards are also part of the dragon tradition. In fact, the largest lizard in the world is known as the Komodo dragon; its toxic bite may have contributed to legends of the dangers of being nipped by a mythical beast. Smaller lizards like the bearded dragon and the flying dragon carry the draconic name and have rather fabulous appearances, though they're much more harmless compared to their giant cousin.

The third group to add to the dragon legends includes alligators, crocodiles, and their kin. These delightfully prehistoric creatures don't need much help to inspire legends of fearsome beasts that would give even the bravest knight a good fight—or bestow power upon an emperor. With their ridged skin, their sharp teeth, and the enormous size of older individuals, they already look the part!

Speaking of prehistoric, dinosaurs—or, rather, their bones—added even more substance to the dragon tales. Many people believed that fossilized skeletons truly were the remains of dragons, and it wasn't until the dawn of paleontology that there was a substantive effort to show that, no, these were merely extinct creatures.

Of course, we do have one group of dinosaurs today: the birds. And in fact some dragons do have more birdlike features, such as feathers or beaks. With the popularity of dragons in modern art, the internet holds a treasure trove of dragons who resemble everything from sparrows to eagles, as well as nonbirds like cats and wolves.

Griffins and Hippogriffs

Speaking of animals with a mixed heritage, what about the griffin? Normally depicted as half eagle, half lion, it sometimes ends up confused with the hippogriff, who trades out the lion half for horse. Even images of traditional griffins sometimes give the animal cloven hooves on the back legs instead of paws.

Unsurprisingly, the lion, eagle, and horse are all contributors to legends of these animals. One eagle species in particular should be given attention: the crowned eagle. This majestic African bird has a crest of feathers on top of its head that, when raised, look very much like a pair of horse ears. When Europeans came to South America, they discovered a similarly crested bird, the harpy eagle. Both of these are notable contributors to griffin and hippogriff legends.

Phoenixes

A bird that dies on a funeral pyre and then rises up from the ashes as good as new is a legend that has persisted in several cultures. The earliest version is the Egyptian Bennu, a powerful solar bird spirit favored by Ra and Atum and instrumental in the creation of the world. And like other phoenixes, it periodically rebirthed itself through fire.

The Bennu was likely inspired by a now-extinct heron that was once found throughout the Arabian peninsula. And in fact the hieroglyphs associated with this sacred bird are quite heron-like in appearance. However, the Pyramid Texts, a collection of Old Egyptian writings, say that the Bennu was in fact a western yellow wagtail, a much smaller songbird that can be still found today.

Mermaids

Mermaids are a huge fad right now, with thousands of people worldwide donning artificial tails so that they can swim about in the water as half-human, half-fish beauties. The real-life counterparts to these beings are a bit less romantic, though no less amazing. Manatees and dugongs are aquatic beings whose closest relatives are elephants. They look a bit like walruses with no tusks, and they have gently rounded bodies with flippers and a tail that they slowly sway to move from place to place. It takes some imagination to see them as beautiful women from the waist up, but given that we can create dragons from grass snakes, anything is possible!

It's also possible that dolphins may have contributed to mermaid tales, especially as they're a bit more wide-ranging than their manatee neighbors. So it may be worth it to work that animal into your mermaid lore as well!

How to Work with the Totems

So now that you know some of the physical animals associated with fantastic beings, how can you bring these two forces together in your spiritual work? Here are some ideas:

Get to know both the physical and mythical creatures in detail. Research the natural history of the physical animals, where they live, how they behave, what they eat, and how else they're adapted to their

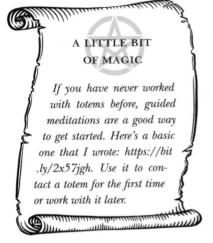

ecosystems. Study up on mythology associated with both the physical and fantastic animals in question: for example, myths about unicorns and legends about horses. Then consider ways in which the physical animal may have influenced stories about the mythical one, like how the gemsbok's appearance from the side could have made people think that it truly was a one-horned deer-horse-goat-like being.

Work with the totems of both the physical and fantastic beings. Get to know Dragon in detail, but also work with Snake and Komodo Dragon, among others. You can even work with the totems of the extinct dinosaurs whose bones inspired draconic legends. As you work with all of them, note how they are similar and ways in which they're different. You may find that there are a lot of common threads in what they have to show you, but that they each have their unique emphasis.

Work with them in ritual, both together and separately. For example, you might call on Phoenix for help with transitioning to a new stage of your life and doing a rite of passage in which you symbolically burn away the old and are reborn as the new. Later you may ask Eagle to guide you in expanding your view of your world, and being able to get a big-picture view of life. Then you could work with both of these totems in a ritual to help you solidify your intent to move forward on a new project or endeavor that you now feel comfortable starting.

Ask the fantastic totems if there are any other physical animals that they feel connected to. You might be surprised who their allies are! Then ask them to introduce you to them to expand your circle of spiritual guides.

You'll notice that I didn't include any meanings for any of the totems. That's because, just like you and me, totems are multifaceted, complex beings who can't be summarized in a few sentences. More importantly, what a particular totem wants to teach me may be completely different from what it wants to teach you. So get to know them as individuals, not stereotypes.

Giving Back to the Totems

Unicorns are not an endangered species, but rhinos are critically threatened by poaching and habitat loss. One of the very best things you can do for any totem is to help its physical counterparts. Here are a few ways to do that:

Donate money to nonprofit organizations working to protect the animals and their habitats. There are a lot of organizations that focus on a specific species or ecosystem, as well as those doing more widespread work. Research them carefully before donating; www .charitynavigator.org can help you assess the effectiveness of those based in the United States, at least. You don't have to donate an entire paycheck, either. Even a few dollars can make a difference!

Volunteer with a local organization working toward habitat restoration. Even if there aren't any manatees or lions where you are, you can still help the creatures who are native to your area. And who knows? An improved wilderness may be just what a deer or mountain lion needs to feel more comfortable, which could make Unicorn or Griffin happy!

Contact elected officials to tell them to support legislation that protects wildlife and their habitats. This isn't just limited to your own representatives, though they certainly could use your words. You can also contact officials in other states or countries to tell them that it's important to you and other people that rare species and the places they live are protected so that everyone can enjoy them.

Try to live lightly on the earth. Everything is connected, and pollution created where you are could affect an ecosystem thousands of miles away. For example, try to cut down on the plastic in your life. Not only does it not biodegrade, but thousands of animals die every year from eating plastic they mistake for food. And there's a huge island of plastic in the middle of the Pacific Ocean made entirely of our garbage. So just by buying biodegradable items instead of plastic ones, you could make a difference for places you've never even seen.

These are just a few suggestions for ways to work with mythical totems and their physical kindred. The more you work with them, the more ideas you'll come up with for bringing them into your life.

Earth Goddess Dreaming: A Paper Sachet of She Who Dreams

Silver RavenWolf

I created the Earth Goddess Dreaming design to work for you as a friend, helper, mentor, and confidante. She is of the earth, and her power is all-encompassing on this planet as well as the realms and pathways associated with all of earth energy. I use the design in meditation and magick, in sacred drumming meditation, in rituals to honor nature and all the elements, and to work productively to find solutions to everyday problems. The image took shape in my mind after a drumming circle as I was contemplating a pattern for connecting with nature—a guide (if you will) of sacred earth love.

The Earth Goddess Dreaming design lends itself well to a variety of media, including paper, felt, wood, and clay. This article focuses on creating a paper sachet; however, feel free to let your imagination soar and utilize She Who Dreams (the name I have given her) in a way that will be most advantageous to you. The archetype helps you "dream" (think, contemplate, meditate, envision, activate) your desires into being. She walks between the worlds as a benefactor to your well-being in this lifetime. She sees all, she helps all, she heals all, she loves all. I have found that the design responds best to air magick actions like rattling, drumming, singing—to me the vibrations you create merge with She Who Dreams and casts a sweet web to capture and bring your desires to fruition. I have also discovered profound peace when holding the image, particularly while working outdoors.

She Who Dreams has her hands on her hips, a stance that is familiar to many of us as a universal gesture that the individual is ready to move forward, desires action, and won't be thwarted easily. Rather than passive, She Who Dreams is assertive, ready to embrace the challenge! Her heart is the center of the earth and

*Dreaming Goddess of the Lower World of Pure Nature
for Shamanic Dreaming Pattern*

the fan on her belly relates to the four elements. The large circle is her creative power and the three dots symbolize the alignment of the three selves: the higher self, the spiritual self, and the carbon (material) self. Her hair has several associations: the waves of water/energy, personal growth, and the creative sharing of the self through mental, physical, or spiritual venues.

You may wish to begin using She Who Dreams by meeting her in meditation or a personally designed ritual that you create. One of my favorite vision quests utilizes a very large tree with a human-size entrance at the base. Once inside the tree, there is a comfortable, sacred space with a sweet, reflective pool, a small sacred fire, and unending exotic flowers! I take time to smell the light, scented air, touch the vegetation, and run my fingers over the mossy ground. Relaxing and breathing deeply is essential to fine-tune yourself to this doorway to divine nature. There are also large, sacred stones where I can sit and relax while gazing into the pool. Often She Who Dreams escorts power animals into my sacred circle when I have asked for help on an issue. In other instances, she clears the way, removing stagnation, blocks, or barriers, whether they are mine or belong to another person, while I sing or drum.

Make a Paper Sachet

Once you have met She Who Dreams in meditation, you are ready to use the design as you wish. You can copy the Dreaming Goddess of the Lower World of Pure Nature for Shamanic Dreaming pattern (see page 103) on a photocopier, trace the design, or even take a photo of it to print out on your computer. Set your intent with a simple statement that is formulated in a way that reinforces that you already have what you are requesting. Feel free to color your copy with colored pencils, markers or art pens. As you add layers of color, whisper your intent over the drawing, ensuring that the moisture in your breath touches the paper. The mindset of She Who Dreams is that anything is possible—there are no barriers to obtaining your desire. The intent of She Who Dreams is what you make it to be. If you turn the figure upside down, you will see that the inner sigil mimics the hands-on-hips stance.

For your sachet, simply photocopy the design and then adjust the image to fit the size of paper you wish to use. Color your image while whispering your intent, or leave it in black and white form. Add a small amount of herbs to the center of the design, and roll the paper with the herbs either toward you (to draw something to you) or away from you (to banish), then tie it with a purple ribbon. I use purple to represent the "higher principle." You can choose a different color of ribbon if you like. You can also put the design on a paper envelope filled with dried herbs and a petition or photograph of your choice tucked inside.

One of my favorite techniques is to draw She Who Dreams on a thin paper plate or 8.5 × 11-inch piece of paper, then cover the image with salt or sugar (you choose). Take a spirit walk. As you walk, move with the mindset that anything is possible and repeat your intent under your breath. Collect small, interesting objects that Spirit guides you to, such as a shell, an unusual rock, a feather, and so on. (Spirit walks are also covered in my book *The Witching Hour.*)

When you return home, draw a sigil in the salt or sugar using a stick, skewer, or knife that represents your intent. It is okay to just let go and draw any design, allowing your subconscious to choose what is right. Whisper, sing, or hum as you do this. Place the found objects on the design. Fold up the plate or paper and burn it safely in an outdoor ritual fire. The flames convert your intention into a living being. The smoke sends that living being to the essence of Spirit, where it will return, in time, to the physical plane in the manner in which you envisioned (or better). Feel free to use any chant, charm, or type of magickal or ritual operation that meets your needs. There is no wrong way to use She Who Dreams. All will be as it should be.

Recommended Herbs

Here are a few of my favorite herbal blends that you might like to use when working with She Who Dreams:

Brilliant Beauty: For workings of beauty and love, use lavender, chamomile, calendula, catnip, juniper berries, jasmine flowers, peppermint, lemon verbena, lemon peel, comfrey leaf, and rose petals. This can also be steeped in warm water and used for facial revitalization.

Fire Web Protection: For workings of personal or family protection, try dragon's blood resin, nettles, ginger, cinnamon, galangal, cloves, and brick dust.

Gratitude: For workings of honor, thanksgiving, and gratitude, use cherry seeds (washed and dried), *Ginkgo biloba*, holy basil, hawthorn flowers, nettles, red clover, and rose petals.

Harmony: For workings of peaceful and sympathetic vibrations, use white birch, hawthorn flowers, St. John's wort, cornflower, holy basil, and eggshell.

Muse: For all manner of creativity, try lime peel, coconut shreds, *Ginkgo biloba*, gotu kola, rosemary, peppermint, lemongrass, ashwagandha, and blue cornflower petals.

Sacred Cleanse: For workings of banishing illness and negativity, use lavender, sweetgrass, white sage, and palo santo.

Shaman's Journey: For vision questing, dreaming, drumming and the shaman's journey, use jasmine flowers, rose petals, holy basil, orange peel, calendula, ginger, hibiscus petals, lavender, and lemongrass.

2020 Almanac

The Date

The date is used in numerological calculations that govern magical rites. Below is a calendar for 2020.

JANUARY

			1	2	3	4
5	6	7	8	9	10	11
12	13	14	15	16	17	18
19	20	21	22	23	24	25
26	27	28	29	30	31	

FEBRUARY

						1
2	3	4	5	6	7	8
9	10	11	12	13	14	15
16	17	18	19	20	21	22
23	24	25	26	27	28	29

MARCH

1	2	3	4	5	6	7
8	9	10	11	12	13	14
15	16	17	18	19	20	21
22	23	24	25	26	27	28
29	30	31				

APRIL

			1	2	3	4
5	6	7	8	9	10	11
12	13	14	15	16	17	18
19	20	21	22	23	24	25
26	27	28	29	30		

MAY

					1	2
3	4	5	6	7	8	9
10	11	12	13	14	15	16
17	18	19	20	21	22	23
24	25	26	27	28	29	30
31						

JUNE

	1	2	3	4	5	6
7	8	9	10	11	12	13
14	15	16	17	18	19	20
21	22	23	24	25	26	27
28	29	30				

JULY

			1	2	3	4
5	6	7	8	9	10	11
12	13	14	15	16	17	18
19	20	21	22	23	24	25
26	27	28	29	30	31	

AUGUST

						1
2	3	4	5	6	7	8
9	10	11	12	13	14	15
16	17	18	19	20	21	22
23	24	25	26	27	28	29
30	31					

SEPTEMBER

		1	2	3	4	5
6	7	8	9	10	11	12
13	14	15	16	17	18	19
20	21	22	23	24	25	26
27	28	29	30			

OCTOBER

				1	2	3
4	5	6	7	8	9	10
11	12	13	14	15	16	17
18	19	20	21	22	23	24
25	26	27	28	29	30	31

NOVEMBER

1	2	3	4	5	6	7
8	9	10	11	12	13	14
15	16	17	18	19	20	21
22	23	24	25	26	27	28
29	30					

DECEMBER

		1	2	3	4	5
6	7	8	9	10	11	12
13	14	15	16	17	18	19
20	21	22	23	24	25	26
27	28	29	30	31		

The Day

Each day is ruled by a planet that possesses specific magical influences:

MONDAY (MOON): Peace, sleep, healing, compassion, friends, psychic awareness, purification, and fertility.

TUESDAY (MARS): Passion, sex, courage, aggression, and protection.

WEDNESDAY (MERCURY): The conscious mind, study, travel, divination, and wisdom.

THURSDAY (JUPITER): Expansion, money, prosperity, and generosity.

FRIDAY (VENUS): Love, friendship, reconciliation, and beauty.

SATURDAY (SATURN): Longevity, exorcism, endings, homes, and houses.

SUNDAY (SUN): Healing, spirituality, success, strength, and protection.

The Lunar Phase

The lunar phase is important in determining the best times for magic.

THE WAXING MOON (from the New Moon to the Full) is the ideal time for magic to draw things toward you.

THE FULL MOON is the time of greatest power.

THE WANING MOON (from the Full Moon to the New) is a time for study, meditation, and little magical work (except magic designed to banish harmful energies).

The Moon's Sign

The Moon continuously "moves" through the zodiac, from Aries to Pisces. Each sign possesses its own significance.

ARIES: Good for starting things, but lacks staying power. Things occur rapidly, but quickly pass. People tend to be argumentative and assertive.

TAURUS: Things begun now last the longest, tend to increase in value, and become hard to alter. Brings out appreciation for beauty and sensory experience.

GEMINI: Things begun now are easily changed by outside influence. Time for shortcuts, communication, games, and fun.

CANCER: Stimulates emotional rapport between people. Pinpoints need, supports growth and nurturance. Tends to domestic concerns.

LEO: Draws emphasis to the self, central ideas, or institutions, away from connections with others and other emotional needs. People tend to be melodramatic.

VIRGO: Favors accomplishment of details and commands from higher up. Focuses on health, hygiene, and daily schedules.

LIBRA: Favors cooperation, social activities, beautification of surroundings, balance, and partnership.

SCORPIO: Increases awareness of psychic power. Precipitates psychic crises and ends connections thoroughly. People tend to brood and become secretive.

SAGITTARIUS: Encourages flights of imagination and confidence. This is an adventurous, philosophical, and athletic Moon sign. Favors expansion and growth.

CAPRICORN: Develops strong structure. Focus on traditions, responsibilities, and obligations. A good time to set boundaries and rules.

AQUARIUS: Rebellious energy. Time to break habits and make abrupt changes. Personal freedom and individuality is the focus.

PISCES: The focus is on dreaming, nostalgia, intuition, and psychic impressions. A good time for spiritual or philanthropic activities.

Color and Incense

The color and incense for the day are based on information from *Personal Alchemy* by Amber Wolfe, and relate to the planet that rules each day. This information can be taken into consideration along with other factors when planning works of magic or when blending magic into mundane life. Please note that the incense selections listed are not hard and fast. See page 269 for a list of color correspondences. If you cannot find or do not like the incense listed for the day, choose a similar scent that appeals to you.

Holidays and Festivals

Holidays and festivals and many cultures and nations are listed throughout the year. The exact dates of many ancient festivals are difficult to determine; prevailing data has been used.

Time Zones

The times and dates of all astrological phenomena in this almanac are based on **Eastern Standard Time (EST)**. If you live outside of the Eastern time zone, you will need to make the following adjustments:

PACIFIC STANDARD TIME: Subtract three hours.

MOUNTAIN STANDARD TIME: Subtract two hours.

CENTRAL STANDARD TIME: Subtract one hour.

ALASKA: Subtract four hours.

HAWAII: Subtract five hours.

DAYLIGHT SAVING TIME (ALL ZONES): Add one hour.

Daylight Saving Time begins at 2 am on March 8, 2020 and ends at 2 am on November 1, 2020.

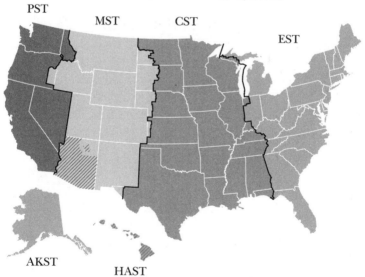

Please refer to a world time zone resource for time adjustments for locations outside the United States.

2020 Sabbats
and Full Moons

January 10	Cancer Full Moon 2:21 pm
February 2	Imbolc
February 9	Leo Full Moon 2:33 am
March 9	Virgo Full Moon 1:48 pm
March 19	Ostara (Spring Equinox)
April 7	Libra Full Moon 10:35 pm
May 1	Beltane
May 7	Scorpio Full Moon 6:45 am
June 5	Sagittarius Full Moon 3:12 pm
June 20	Midsummer (Summer Solstice)
July 5	Capricorn Full Moon 12:44 am
August 1	Lammas
August 3	Aquarius Full Moon 11:59 am
September 2	Pisces Full Moon 1:22 am
September 22	Mabon (Fall Equinox)
October 1	Aries Full Moon 5:05 pm
October 31	Samhain
October 31	Taurus Full Moon 10:49 am
November 30	Gemini Full Moon 4:30 am
December 21	Yule (Winter Solstice)
December 29	Cancer Full Moon 10:28 pm

All times are Eastern Standard Time (EST)
or Eastern Daylight Time (EDT)

2020 Sabbats in the Southern Hemisphere

Because Earth's Northern and Southern Hemispheres experience opposite seasons at any given time, the season-based sabbats listed on the previous page and in this almanac section are not correct for those residing south of the equator. Listed here are the Southern Hemisphere sabbat dates for 2020:

February 1	Lammas
March 19	Mabon (Fall Equinox)
May 1	Samhain
June 20	Yule (Winter Solstice)
August 1	Imbolc
September 22	Ostara (Spring Equinox)
November 1	Beltane
December 21	Midsummer (Summer Solstice)

Birthstone Poetry

Birthstone poetry in the monthly calendar
reprinted from
The Occult and Curative Powers of Precious Stones
by William T. Fernie, M.D.
Harper & Row (1981)

Originally printed in 1907 as
Precious Stones:
For Curative Wear; and Other Remedial Uses;
Likewise the Nobler Metals

January

1 **Wednesday**
New Year's Day • Kwanzaa ends
Waxing Moon
Moon phase: First Quarter
Color: Yellow

Moon Sign: Pisces
Moon enters Aries 11:00 pm
Incense: Marjoram

☾ **Thursday**
First Writing Day (Japanese)
Waxing Moon
Second Quarter 11:45 pm
Color: Turquoise

Moon Sign: Aries
Incense: Jasmine

3 **Friday**
St. Genevieve's Day
Waxing Moon
Moon phase: Second Quarter
Color: Pink

Moon Sign: Aries
Incense: Mint

4 **Saturday**
Kamakura Workers' Festival (Japanese)
Waxing Moon
Moon phase: Second Quarter
Color: Gray

Moon Sign: Aries
Moon enters Taurus 11:15 am
Incense: Pine

5 **Sunday**
Bird Day
Waxing Moon
Moon phase: Second Quarter
Color: Amber

Moon Sign: Taurus
Incense: Juniper

6 **Monday**
Epiphany
Waxing Moon
Moon phase: Second Quarter
Color: Silver

Moon Sign: Taurus
Moon enters Gemini 9:11 pm
Incense: Lily

7 **Tuesday**
Tricolor Day (Italian)
Waxing Moon
Moon phase: Second Quarter
Color: White

Moon Sign: Gemini
Incense: Bayberry

January

8 Wednesday
Midwives' Day (Bulgarian)
Waxing Moon
Moon phase: Second Quarter
Color: Brown

Moon Sign: Gemini
Incense: Honeysuckle

9 Thursday
Feast of the Black Nazarene (Filipino)
Waxing Moon
Moon phase: Second Quarter
Color: Purple

Moon Sign: Gemini
Moon enters Cancer 3:43 am
Incense: Myrrh

☺ Friday
Feast of St. Leonie Aviat
Waxing Moon
Full Moon 2:21 pm
Color: Rose

Moon Sign: Cancer
Incense: Rose

11 Saturday
Carmentalia (Roman)
Waning Moon
Moon phase: Third Quarter
Color: Blue

Moon Sign: Cancer
Moon enters Leo 7:16 am
Incense: Sage

12 Sunday
Revolution Day (Tanzanian)
Waning Moon
Moon phase: Third Quarter
Color: Orange

Moon Sign: Leo
Incense: Frankincense

13 Monday
Twentieth Day (Norwegian)
Waning Moon
Moon phase: Third Quarter
Color: White

Moon Sign: Leo
Moon enters Virgo 9:06 am
Incense: Hyssop

14 Tuesday
Feast of the Ass (French)
Waning Moon
Moon phase: Third Quarter
Color: Black

Moon Sign: Virgo
Incense: Ylang-ylang

January

15 Wednesday
Korean Alphabet Day
Waning Moon
Moon phase: Third Quarter
Color: Yellow

Moon Sign: Virgo
Moon enters Libra 10:43 am
Incense: Lavender

16 Thursday
Teachers' Day (Thai)
Waning Moon
Moon phase: Third Quarter
Color: Crimson

Moon Sign: Libra
Incense: Clove

◑ Friday
St. Anthony's Day (Mexican)
Waning Moon
Fourth Quarter 7:58 am
Color: Purple

Moon Sign: Libra
Moon enters Scorpio 1:20 pm
Incense: Thyme

18 Saturday
Feast of St. Athanasius
Waning Moon
Moon phase: Fourth Quarter
Color: Black

Moon Sign: Scorpio
Incense: Rue

19 Sunday
Edgar Allan Poe's birthday
Waning Moon
Moon phase: Fourth Quarter
Color: Gold

Moon Sign: Scorpio
Moon enters Sagittarius 5:41 pm
Incense: Marigold

20 Monday
Martin Luther King Jr. Day
Waning Moon
Moon phase: Fourth Quarter
Color: Ivory

Moon Sign: Sagittarius
Sun enters Aquarius 9:55 am
Incense: Clary sage

21 Tuesday
St. Agnes's Day
Waning Moon
Moon phase: Fourth Quarter
Color: Maroon

Moon Sign: Sagittarius
Incense: Geranium

22 Wednesday

St. Vincent's Day (French)
Waning Moon
Moon phase: Fourth Quarter
Color: Topaz

Moon Sign: Sagittarius
Moon enters Capricorn 12:00 am
Incense: Lilac

---

23 Thursday

Feast of St. Ildefonsus
Waning Moon
Moon phase: Fourth Quarter
Color: Green

Moon Sign: Capricorn
Incense: Nutmeg

☽ Friday

Alasitas Fair (Bolivian)
Waning Moon
New Moon 4:42 pm
Color: Coral

Moon Sign: Capricorn
Moon enters Aquarius 8:20 am
Incense: Violet

---

25 Saturday

Lunar New Year (Rat)
Waxing Moon
Moon phase: First Quarter
Color: Gray

Moon Sign: Aquarius
Incense: Sandalwood

---

26 Sunday

Australia Day
Waxing Moon
Moon phase: First Quarter
Color: Yellow

Moon Sign: Aquarius
Moon enters Pisces 6:44 pm
Incense: Heliotrope

---

27 Monday

Holocaust Remembrance Day
Waxing Moon
Moon phase: First Quarter
Color: Lavender

Moon Sign: Pisces
Incense: Rosemary

---

28 Tuesday

Up Helly Aa (Scottish)
Waxing Moon
Moon phase: First Quarter
Color: Scarlet

Moon Sign: Pisces
Incense: Ginger

January

29 Wednesday
Feast of St. Gildas
Waxing Moon
Moon phase: First Quarter
Color: White

Moon Sign: Pisces
Moon enters Aries 6:51 am
Incense: Bay laurel

---

30 Thursday
Martyrs' Day (Indian)
Waxing Moon
Moon phase: First Quarter
Color: Purple

Moon Sign: Aries
Incense: Carnation

---

31 Friday
Independence Day (Nauru)
Waxing Moon
Moon phase: First Quarter
Color: Rose

Moon Sign: Aries
Moon enters Taurus 7:28 pm
Incense: Vanilla

January Birthstones

*By her in January born
No gem save Garnets should be worn;
They will ensure her constancy,
True friendship, and fidelity.*

Modern: Garnet   Zodiac (Capricorn): Ruby

February Birthstones

*The February-born shall find
Sincerity, and peace of mind,
Freedom from passion and from care,
If they the Amethyst will wear.*

Modern: Amethyst   Zodiac (Aquarius): Garnet

February

◐ Saturday
St. Brigid's Day (Irish)
Waxing Moon
Second Quarter 8:42 pm
Color: Indigo

Moon Sign: Taurus
Incense: Ivy

---

2 Sunday
Imbolc • Groundhog Day
Waxing Moon
Moon phase: Second Quarter
Color: Gold

Moon Sign: Taurus
Incense: Almond

---

3 Monday
St. Blaise's Day
Waxing Moon
Moon phase: Second Quarter
Color: Gray

Moon Sign: Taurus
Moon enters Gemini 6:29 am
Incense: Neroli

---

4 Tuesday
Independence Day (Sri Lankan)
Waxing Moon
Moon phase: Second Quarter
Color: Red

Moon Sign: Gemini
Incense: Bayberry

---

5 Wednesday
Constitution Day (Mexican)
Waxing Moon
Moon phase: Second Quarter
Color: White

Moon Sign: Gemini
Moon enters Cancer 2:03 pm
Incense: Honeysuckle

---

6 Thursday
Bob Marley's birthday (Jamaican)
Waxing Moon
Moon phase: Second Quarter
Color: Green

Moon Sign: Cancer
Incense: Apricot

---

7 Friday
Feast of St. Richard the Pilgrim
Waxing Moon
Moon phase: Second Quarter
Color: Purple

Moon Sign: Cancer
Moon enters Leo 5:45 pm
Incense: Cypress

February

8 Saturday
Lantern Festival (Chinese)
Waxing Moon
Moon phase: Second Quarter
Color: Blue

Moon Sign: Leo
Incense: Patchouli

Sunday
St. Maron's Day (Lebanese)
Waxing Moon
Full Moon 2:33 am
Color: Amber

Moon Sign: Leo
Moon enters Virgo 6:39 pm
Incense: Eucalyptus

---

10 Monday
Feast of St. Scholastica
Waning Moon
Moon phase: Third Quarter
Color: Ivory

Moon Sign: Virgo
Incense: Hyssop

---

11 Tuesday
National Foundation Day (Japanese)
Waning Moon
Moon phase: Third Quarter
Color: Scarlet

Moon Sign: Virgo
Moon enters Libra 6:37 pm
Incense: Cedar

---

12 Wednesday
Abraham Lincoln's birthday
Waning Moon
Moon phase: Third Quarter
Color: Brown

Moon Sign: Libra
Incense: Lilac

---

13 Thursday
Parentalia
Waning Moon
Moon phase: Third Quarter
Color: Turquoise

Moon Sign: Libra
Moon enters Scorpio 7:37 pm
Incense: Balsam

---

14 Friday
Valentine's Day
Waning Moon
Moon phase: Third Quarter
Color: Coral

Moon Sign: Scorpio
Incense: Alder

February

Saturday
Susan B. Anthony Day
Waning Moon
Fourth Quarter 5:17 pm
Color: Gray

Moon Sign: Scorpio
Moon enters Sagittarius 11:07 pm
Incense: Magnolia

---

16 Sunday
Feast of St. Juliana of Nicomedia
Waning Moon
Moon phase: Fourth Quarter
Color: Orange

Moon Sign: Sagittarius
Incense: Hyacinth

---

17 Monday
Presidents' Day
Waning Moon
Moon phase: Fourth Quarter
Color: White

Moon Sign: Sagittarius
Incense: Narcissus

---

18 Tuesday
St. Bernadette's Third Vision
Waning Moon
Moon phase: Fourth Quarter
Color: Black

Moon Sign: Sagittarius
Sun enters Pisces 11:57 pm
Moon enters Capricorn 5:37 am
Incense: Cinnamon

---

19 Wednesday
Flag Day (Turkmenian)
Waning Moon
Moon phase: Fourth Quarter
Color: Yellow

Moon Sign: Capricorn
Incense: Marjoram

---

20 Thursday
World Day of Social Justice
Waning Moon
Moon phase: Fourth Quarter
Color: Purple

Moon Sign: Capricorn
Moon enters Aquarius 2:42 pm
Incense: Mulberry

---

21 Friday
Maha Shivaratri
Waning Moon
Moon phase: Fourth Quarter
Color: Pink

Moon Sign: Aquarius
Incense: Thyme

22 Saturday

Caristia (Roman)
Waning Moon
Moon phase: Fourth Quarter
Color: Black

Moon Sign: Aquarius
Incense: Pine

Sunday

Mashramani Festival (Guyana)
Waning Moon
New Moon 10:32 am
Color: Yellow

Moon Sign: Aquarius
Moon enters Pisces 1:37 am
Incense: Marigold

24 Monday

Blue Dragon Festival (Chinese)
Waxing Moon
Moon phase: First Quarter
Color: Silver

Moon Sign: Pisces
Incense: Lily

25 Tuesday

Mardi Gras (Fat Tuesday)
Waxing Moon
Moon phase: First Quarter
Color: Maroon

Moon Sign: Pisces
Moon enters Aries 1:47 pm
Incense: Ylang-ylang

26 Wednesday

Ash Wednesday
Waxing Moon
Moon phase: First Quarter
Color: Topaz

Moon Sign: Aries
Incense: Lavender

27 Thursday

Independence Day (Dominican)
Waxing Moon
Moon phase: First Quarter
Color: White

Moon Sign: Aries
Incense: Clove

28 Friday

Kalevala Day (Finnish)
Waxing Moon
Moon phase: First Quarter
Color: Rose

Moon Sign: Aries
Moon enters Taurus 2:30 am
Incense: Orchid

March

29 Saturday
Leap Day
Waxing Moon
Moon phase: First Quarter
Color: Brown

Moon Sign: Taurus
Incense: Ivy

---

1 Sunday
Matronalia (Roman)
Waxing Moon
Moon phase: First Quarter
Color: Yellow

Moon Sign: Taurus
Moon enters Gemini 2:21 pm
Incense: Frankincense

◑ **Monday**
Read Across America Day
Waxing Moon
Second Quarter 2:57 pm
Color: Ivory

Moon Sign: Gemini
Incense: Clary sage

---

3 Tuesday
Doll Festival (Japanese)
Waxing Moon
Moon phase: Second Quarter
Color: Black

Moon Sign: Gemini
Moon enters Cancer 11:25 pm
Incense: Basil

---

4 Wednesday
St. Casimir's Fair (Polish and Lithuanian)
Waxing Moon
Moon phase: Second Quarter
Color: Brown

Moon Sign: Cancer
Incense: Bay laurel

---

5 Thursday
Navigium Isidis Festival (Roman)
Waxing Moon
Moon phase: Second Quarter
Color: Purple

Moon Sign: Cancer
Incense: Carnation

---

6 Friday
Alamo Day (Texas)
Waxing Moon
Moon phase: Second Quarter
Color: White

Moon Sign: Cancer
Moon enters Leo 4:27 am
Incense: Rose

March

7 Saturday
Vejovis Festival (Roman)
Waxing Moon
Moon phase: Second Quarter
Color: Black

Moon Sign: Leo
Incense: Sandalwood

---

8 Sunday
International Women's Day
Waxing Moon
Moon phase: Second Quarter
Color: Amber

Moon Sign: Leo
Moon enters Virgo 6:47 am
Incense: Juniper
Daylight Saving Time begins at 2 am

☾ Monday
Teachers' Day (Lebanese)
Waxing Moon
Full Moon 1:48 pm
Color: Lavender

Moon Sign: Virgo
Incense: Neroli

---

10 Tuesday
Purim begins (at sundown on March 9)
Waning Moon
Moon phase: Third Quarter
Color: Red

Moon Sign: Virgo
Moon enters Libra 6:03 am
Incense: Geranium

---

11 Wednesday
Johnny Appleseed Day
Waning Moon
Moon phase: Third Quarter
Color: Yellow

Moon Sign: Libra
Incense: Lilac

---

12 Thursday
Girl Scouts' birthday
Waning Moon
Moon phase: Third Quarter
Color: White

Moon Sign: Libra
Moon enters Scorpio 5:28 am
Incense: Jasmine

---

13 Friday
Feast of St. Leander of Seville
Waning Moon
Moon phase: Third Quarter
Color: Rose

Moon Sign: Scorpio
Incense: Yarrow

March

14 Saturday
Pi Day • Mamuralia (Roman)
Waning Moon
Moon phase: Third Quarter
Color: Blue

Moon Sign: Scorpio
Moon enters Sagittarius 7:09 am
Incense: Sage

---

15 Sunday
Fertility Festival (Japanese)
Waning Moon
Moon phase: Third Quarter
Color: Orange

Moon Sign: Sagittarius
Incense: Eucalyptus

---

16 Monday
St. Urho's Day (Finnish-American)
Waning Moon
Fourth Quarter 5:34 am
Color: Gray

Moon Sign: Sagittarius
Moon enters Capricorn 12:25 pm
Incense: Rosemary

---

17 Tuesday
St. Patrick's Day
Waning Moon
Moon phase: Fourth Quarter
Color: Maroon

Moon Sign: Capricorn
Incense: Cedar

---

18 Wednesday
Sheila's Day (Irish)
Waning Moon
Moon phase: Fourth Quarter
Color: Topaz

Moon Sign: Capricorn
Moon enters Aquarius 9:16 pm
Incense: Marjoram

---

19 Thursday
Ostara • Spring Equinox
Waning Moon
Moon phase: Fourth Quarter
Color: Green

Moon Sign: Aquarius
Sun enters Aries 11:50 pm
Incense: Apricot

---

20 Friday
Denver March Powwow (ends Mar. 22)
Waning Moon
Moon phase: Fourth Quarter
Color: Purple

Moon Sign: Aquarius
Incense: Vanilla

March

21 Saturday
Harmony Day (Australian)
Waning Moon
Moon phase: Fourth Quarter
Color: Indigo

Moon Sign: Aquarius
Moon enters Pisces 8:33 am
Incense: Rue

---

22 Sunday
World Water Day
Waning Moon
Moon phase: Fourth Quarter
Color: Gold

Moon Sign: Pisces
Incense: Almond

---

23 Monday
Pakistan Day
Waning Moon
Moon phase: Fourth Quarter
Color: Silver

Moon Sign: Pisces
Moon enters Aries 8:58 pm
Incense: Hyssop

Tuesday
Day of Blood (Roman)
Waning Moon
New Moon 5:28 am
Color: Gray

Moon Sign: Aries
Incense: Ginger

---

25 Wednesday
Tolkien Reading Day
Waxing Moon
Moon phase: First Quarter
Color: White

Moon Sign: Aries
Incense: Honeysuckle

---

26 Thursday
Prince Kuhio Day (Hawaiian)
Waxing Moon
Moon phase: First Quarter
Color: Turquoise

Moon Sign: Aries
Moon enters Taurus 9:37 am
Incense: Myrrh

---

27 Friday
World Theatre Day
Waxing Moon
Moon phase: First Quarter
Color: Coral

Moon Sign: Taurus
Incense: Mint

March

28 Saturday

Weed Appreciation Day
Waxing Moon
Moon phase: First Quarter
Color: Gray

Moon Sign: Taurus
Moon enters Gemini 9:38 pm
Incense: Magnolia

29 Sunday

Feast of St. Eustace of Luxeuil
Waxing Moon
Moon phase: First Quarter
Color: Amber

Moon Sign: Gemini
Incense: Heliotrope

30 Monday

Seward's Day (Alaskan)
Waxing Moon
Moon phase: First Quarter
Color: White

Moon Sign: Gemini
Incense: Lily

31 Tuesday

César Chavez Day
Waxing Moon
Moon phase: First Quarter
Color: Scarlet

Moon Sign: Gemini
Moon enters Cancer 7:43 am
Incense: Geranium

March Birthstones

Who in this world of ours, her eyes
In March first opens, shall be wise.
In days of peril, firm and brave,
And wear a Bloodstone to her grave.

Modern: Aquamarine
Zodiac (Pisces): Amethyst

April

☽ Wednesday
All Fools' Day • April Fools' Day
Waxing Moon
Second Quarter 6:21 am
Color: Topaz

Moon Sign: Cancer
Incense: Lavender

---

2 Thursday
The Battle of Flowers (French)
Waxing Moon
Moon phase: Second Quarter
Color: Green

Moon Sign: Cancer
Moon enters Leo 2:26 pm
Incense: Nutmeg

---

3 Friday
Feast of St. Mary of Egypt
Waxing Moon
Moon phase: Second Quarter
Color: Pink

Moon Sign: Leo
Incense: Orchid

---

4 Saturday
Tomb-Sweeping Day (Chinese)
Waxing Moon
Moon phase: Second Quarter
Color: Blue

Moon Sign: Leo
Moon enters Virgo 5:18 pm
Incense: Sage

---

5 Sunday
Palm Sunday
Waxing Moon
Moon phase: Second Quarter
Color: Yellow

Moon Sign: Virgo
Incense: Marigold

---

6 Monday
Tartan Day
Waxing Moon
Moon phase: Second Quarter
Color: Gray

Moon Sign: Virgo
Moon enters Libra 5:16 pm
Incense: Hyssop

☺ Tuesday
Motherhood and Beauty Day (Armenian)
Waxing Moon
Full Moon 10:35 pm
Color: White

Moon Sign: Libra
Incense: Cinnamon

April

8 Wednesday

Buddha's birthday
Waning Moon
Moon phase: Third Quarter
Color: Brown

Moon Sign: Libra
Moon enters Scorpio 4:17 pm
Incense: Lilac

9 Thursday

Passover begins (at sundown on April 8)
Waning Moon
Moon phase: Third Quarter
Color: Crimson

Moon Sign: Scorpio
Incense: Mulberry

10 Friday

Good Friday
Waning Moon
Moon phase: Third Quarter
Color: Rose

Moon Sign: Scorpio
Moon enters Sagittarius 4:35 pm
Incense: Violet

11 Saturday

Juan Santamaría Day (Costa Rican)
Waning Moon
Moon phase: Third Quarter
Color: Indigo

Moon Sign: Sagittarius
Incense: Sandalwood

12 Sunday

Easter
Waning Moon
Moon phase: Third Quarter
Color: Gold

Moon Sign: Sagittarius
Moon enters Capricorn 8:05 pm
Incense: Hyacinth

13 Monday

Thai New Year (ends April 15)
Waning Moon
Moon phase: Third Quarter
Color: Ivory

Moon Sign: Capricorn
Incense: Neroli

◑ Tuesday

Black Day (South Korean)
Waning Moon
Fourth Quarter 6:56 pm
Color: Red

Moon Sign: Capricorn
Incense: Bayberry

April

15 Wednesday
Fordicidia (Roman)
Waning Moon
Moon phase: Fourth Quarter
Color: Yellow

Moon Sign: Capricorn
Moon enters Aquarius 3:37 am
Incense: Bay laurel

16 Thursday
Passover ends
Waning Moon
Moon phase: Fourth Quarter
Color: Turquoise

Moon Sign: Aquarius
Incense: Clove

17 Friday
Orthodox Good Friday
Waning Moon
Moon phase: Fourth Quarter
Color: Coral

Moon Sign: Aquarius
Moon enters Pisces 2:29 pm
Incense: Orchid

18 Saturday
International Day for Monuments and Sites
Waning Moon
Moon phase: Fourth Quarter
Color: Brown

Moon Sign: Pisces
Incense: Patchouli

19 Sunday
Orthodox Easter
Waning Moon
Moon phase: Fourth Quarter
Color: Amber

Moon Sign: Pisces
Sun enters Taurus 10:45 am
Incense: Almond

20 Monday
Sechseläuten (Swiss)
Waning Moon
Moon phase: Fourth Quarter
Color: Gray

Moon Sign: Pisces
Moon enters Aries 3:00 am
Incense: Clary sage

21 Tuesday
Tiradentes Day (Brazilian)
Waning Moon
Moon phase: Fourth Quarter
Color: Black

Moon Sign: Aries
Incense: Basil

Wednesday
Earth Day
Waning Moon
New Moon 10:26 pm
Color: White

Moon Sign: Aries
Moon enters Taurus 3:36 pm
Incense: Marjoram

---

23 Thursday
Ramadan begins
Waxing Moon
Moon phase: First Quarter
Color: Green

Moon Sign: Taurus
Incense: Balsam

---

24 Friday
St. Mark's Eve
Waxing Moon
Moon phase: First Quarter
Color: Purple

Moon Sign: Taurus
Incense: Cypress

---

25 Saturday
Robigalia (Roman)
Waxing Moon
Moon phase: First Quarter
Color: Black

Moon Sign: Taurus
Moon enters Gemini 3:20 am
Incense: Pine

---

26 Sunday
Chernobyl Remembrance Day (Belarusian)
Waxing Moon
Moon phase: First Quarter
Color: Yellow

Moon Sign: Gemini
Incense: Frankincense

---

27 Monday
Freedom Day (South African)
Waxing Moon
Moon phase: First Quarter
Color: Silver

Moon Sign: Gemini
Moon enters Cancer 1:28 pm
Incense: Narcissus

---

28 Tuesday
Floralia (Roman)
Waxing Moon
Moon phase: First Quarter
Color: Scarlet

Moon Sign: Cancer
Incense: Geranium

April

29 Wednesday
Showa Day (Japanese)
Waxing Moon
Moon phase: First Quarter
Color: Brown

Moon Sign: Cancer
Moon enters Leo 9:06 pm
Incense: Honeysuckle

 Thursday
Walpurgis Night • May Eve
Waxing Moon
Second Quarter 4:38 pm
Color: Purple

Moon Sign: Leo
Incense: Jasmine

April Birthstones

She who from April dates her years,
Diamonds shall wear, lest bitter tears
For vain repentance flow; this stone
Emblem for innocence is known.

Modern: Diamond
Zodiac (Aries): Bloodstone

May

1 Friday
Beltane • May Day
Waxing Moon
Moon phase: Second Quarter
Color: Rose

Moon Sign: Leo
Incense: Thyme

2 Saturday
National Education Day (Indonesian)
Waxing Moon
Moon phase: Second Quarter
Color: Brown

Moon Sign: Leo
Moon enters Virgo 1:35 am
Incense: Ivy

3 Sunday
Roodmas
Waxing Moon
Moon phase: Second Quarter
Color: Gold

Moon Sign: Virgo
Incense: Almond

4 Monday
Star Wars Day
Waxing Moon
Moon phase: Second Quarter
Color: Ivory

Moon Sign: Virgo
Moon enters Libra 3:09 am
Incense: Rosemary

5 Tuesday
Cinco de Mayo (Mexican)
Waxing Moon
Moon phase: Second Quarter
Color: Red

Moon Sign: Libra
Incense: Cinnamon

6 Wednesday
Martyrs' Day (Lebanese and Syrian)
Waxing Moon
Moon phase: Second Quarter
Color: Topaz

Moon Sign: Libra
Moon enters Scorpio 3:05 am
Incense: Bay laurel

☺ Thursday
Pilgrimage of St. Nicholas (Italian)
Waxing Moon
Full Moon 6:45 am
Color: Green

Moon Sign: Scorpio
Incense: Apricot

May

8 **Friday**
White Lotus Day (Theosophical)
Waning Moon
Moon phase: Third Quarter
Color: White

Moon Sign: Scorpio
Moon enters Sagittarius 3:15 am
Incense: Mint

---

9 **Saturday**
Lemuria (Roman)
Waning Moon
Moon phase: Third Quarter
Color: Blue

Moon Sign: Sagittarius
Incense: Magnolia

---

10 **Sunday**
Mother's Day
Waning Moon
Moon phase: Third Quarter
Color: Orange

Moon Sign: Sagittarius
Moon enters Capricorn 5:39 am
Incense: Eucalyptus

---

11 **Monday**
Ukai season opens (Japanese)
Waning Moon
Moon phase: Third Quarter
Color: Lavender

Moon Sign: Capricorn
Incense: Neroli

---

12 **Tuesday**
Florence Nightingale's birthday
Waning Moon
Moon phase: Third Quarter
Color: White

Moon Sign: Capricorn
Moon enters Aquarius 11:39 am
Incense: Cedar

---

13 **Wednesday**
Pilgrimage to Fátima (Portuguese)
Waning Moon
Moon phase: Third Quarter
Color: Yellow

Moon Sign: Aquarius
Incense: Lavender

○ **Thursday**
Carabao Festival (Spanish)
Waning Moon
Fourth Quarter 10:03 am
Color: Turquoise

Moon Sign: Aquarius
Moon enters Pisces 9:24 pm
Incense: Carnation

May

15 Friday
Festival of St. Dymphna
Waning Moon
Moon phase: Fourth Quarter
Color: Pink

Moon Sign: Pisces
Incense: Vanilla

16 Saturday
St. Honoratus's Day
Waning Moon
Moon phase: Fourth Quarter
Color: Gray

Moon Sign: Pisces
Incense: Rue

17 Sunday
Norwegian Constitution Day
Waning Moon
Moon phase: Fourth Quarter
Color: Yellow

Moon Sign: Pisces
Moon enters Aries 9:36 am
Incense: Hyacinth

18 Monday
Victoria Day (Canadian)
Waning Moon
Moon phase: Fourth Quarter
Color: Gray

Moon Sign: Aries
Incense: Lily

19 Tuesday
Mother's Day (Kyrgyzstani)
Waning Moon
Moon phase: Fourth Quarter
Color: Black

Moon Sign: Aries
Moon enters Taurus 10:10 pm
Incense: Ylang-ylang

20 Wednesday
Feast of St. Aurea of Ostia
Waning Moon
Moon phase: Fourth Quarter
Color: White

Moon Sign: Taurus
Sun enters Gemini 9:49 am
Incense: Majoram

21 Thursday
Navy Day (Chilean)
Waning Moon
Moon phase: Fourth Quarter
Color: Crimson

Moon Sign: Taurus
Incense: Balsam

May

Friday
Harvey Milk Day (Californian)
Waning Moon
New Moon 1:39 pm
Color: Rose

Moon Sign: Taurus
Moon enters Gemini 9:36 am
Incense: Rose

---

23 Saturday
Ramadan ends
Waxing Moon
Moon phase: First Quarter
Color: Blue

Moon Sign: Gemini
Incense: Sandalwood

---

24 Sunday
Education and Culture Day (Bulgarian)
Waxing Moon
Moon phase: First Quarter
Color: Amber

Moon Sign: Gemini
Moon enters Cancer 7:09 pm
Incense: Heliotrope

---

25 Monday
Memorial Day
Waxing Moon
Moon phase: First Quarter
Color: Silver

Moon Sign: Cancer
Incense: Clary sage

---

26 Tuesday
Pepys's Commemoration (English)
Waxing Moon
Moon phase: First Quarter
Color: Scarlet

Moon Sign: Cancer
Incense: Ginger

---

27 Wednesday
Feast of St. Bede the Venerable
Waxing Moon
Moon phase: First Quarter
Color: Brown

Moon Sign: Cancer
Moon enters Leo 2:33 am
Incense: Honeysuckle

---

28 Thursday
St. Germain's Day
Waxing Moon
Moon phase: First Quarter
Color: White

Moon Sign: Leo
Incense: Myrrh

May

◐ **Friday**
Shavuot (begins at sundown on May 28)
Waxing Moon
Second Quarter 11:30 pm
Color: Purple

Moon Sign: Leo
Moon enters Virgo 7:40 am
Incense: Alder

---

30 **Saturday**
Canary Islands Day
Waxing Moon
Moon phase: Second Quarter
Color: Black

Moon Sign: Virgo
Incense: Sage

---

31 **Sunday**
Visitation of Mary
Waxing Moon
Moon phase: Second Quarter
Color: Orange

Moon Sign: Virgo
Moon enters Libra 10:38 am
Incense: Juniper

May Birthstones

Who first beholds the light of day,
In spring's sweet flowery month of May,
And wears an Emerald all her life,
Shall be a loved, and happy wife.

Modern: Emerald
Zodiac (Taurus): Sapphire

June

♊

1 **Monday**
Dayak Harvest Festival (Malaysian)
Waxing Moon
Moon phase: Second Quarter
Color: Lavender

Moon Sign: Libra
Incense: Rosemary

---

2 **Tuesday**
Republic Day (Italian)
Waxing Moon
Moon phase: Second Quarter
Color: Red

Moon Sign: Libra
Moon enters Scorpio 12:06 pm
Incense: Cedar

---

3 **Wednesday**
Feast of St. Clotilde
Waxing Moon
Moon phase: Second Quarter
Color: White

Moon Sign: Scorpio
Incense: Lilac

---

4 **Thursday**
Flag Day (Estonian)
Waxing Moon
Moon phase: Second Quarter
Color: Purple

Moon Sign: Scorpio
Moon enters Sagittarius 1:17 pm
Incense: Mulberry

☺ **Friday**
Constitution Day (Danish)
Waxing Moon
Full Moon 3:12 pm
Color: Rose

Moon Sign: Sagittarius
Incense: Yarrow

---

6 **Saturday**
National Day of Sweden
Waning Moon
Moon phase: Third Quarter
Color: Gray

Moon Sign: Sagittarius
Moon enters Capricorn 3:44 pm
Incense: Patchouli

---

7 **Sunday**
Vestalia begins (Roman)
Waning Moon
Moon phase: Third Quarter
Color: Yellow

Moon Sign: Capricorn
Incense: Frankincense

June

8 Monday
World Oceans Day
Waning Moon
Moon phase: Third Quarter
Color: White

Moon Sign: Capricorn
Moon enters Aquarius 8:54 pm
Incense: Narcissus

9 Tuesday
Heroes' Day (Ugandan)
Waning Moon
Moon phase: Third Quarter
Color: Maroon

Moon Sign: Aquarius
Incense: Basil

10 Wednesday
Portugal Day
Waning Moon
Moon phase: Third Quarter
Color: Brown

Moon Sign: Aquarius
Incense: Marjoram

11 Thursday
Kamehameha Day (Hawaiian)
Waning Moon
Moon phase: Third Quarter
Color: Green

Moon Sign: Aquarius
Moon enters Pisces 5:32 am
Incense: Jasmine

12 Friday
Independence Day (Filipino)
Waning Moon
Moon phase: Third Quarter
Color: Coral

Moon Sign: Pisces
Incense: Cypress

☽ Saturday
St. Anthony of Padua's Day
Waning Moon
Fourth Quarter 2:24 am
Color: Black

Moon Sign: Pisces
Moon enters Aries 5:03 pm
Incense: Ivy

14 Sunday
Flag Day
Waning Moon
Moon phase: Fourth Quarter
Color: Gold

Moon Sign: Aries
Incense: Marigold

June

15 Monday
Vestalia ends (Roman)
Waning Moon
Moon phase: Fourth Quarter
Color: Gray

Moon Sign: Aries
Incense: Lily

16 Tuesday
Bloomsday (Irish)
Waning Moon
Moon phase: Fourth Quarter
Color: White

Moon Sign: Aries
Moon enters Taurus 5:35 am
Incense: Geranium

17 Wednesday
Bunker Hill Day (Massachusetts)
Waning Moon
Moon phase: Fourth Quarter
Color: Yellow

Moon Sign: Taurus
Incense: Bay laurel

18 Thursday
Waterloo Day (British)
Waning Moon
Moon phase: Fourth Quarter
Color: Crimson

Moon Sign: Taurus
Moon enters Gemini 5:00 pm
Incense: Nutmeg

19 Friday
Juneteenth
Waning Moon
Moon phase: Fourth Quarter
Color: Pink

Moon Sign: Gemini
Incense: Mint

20 Saturday
Litha • Summer Solstice
Waning Moon
Moon phase: Fourth Quarter
Color: Indigo

Moon Sign: Gemini
Sun enters Cancer 5:44 pm
Incense: Sandalwood

☽ Sunday
Father's Day
Waning Moon
New Moon 2:41 am
Color: Orange

Moon Sign: Gemini
Moon enters Cancer 2:02 am
Incense: Eucalyptus

June

22 Monday
Teachers' Day (El Salvadoran)
Waxing Moon
Moon phase: First Quarter
Color: Silver

Moon Sign: Cancer
Incense: Neroli

23 Tuesday
St. John's Eve
Waxing Moon
Moon phase: First Quarter
Color: Scarlet

Moon Sign: Cancer
Moon enters Leo 8:33 am
Incense: Ginger

24 Wednesday
St. John's Day
Waxing Moon
Moon phase: First Quarter
Color: Topaz

Moon Sign: Leo
Incense: Lavender

25 Thursday
Fiesta de Santa Orosia (Spanish)
Waxing Moon
Moon phase: First Quarter
Color: Turquoise

Moon Sign: Leo
Moon enters Virgo 1:05 pm
Incense: Clove

26 Friday
Pied Piper Day (German)
Waxing Moon
Moon phase: First Quarter
Color: White

Moon Sign: Virgo
Incense: Rose

27 Saturday
Seven Sleepers' Day (German)
Waxing Moon
Moon phase: First Quarter
Color: Blue

Moon Sign: Virgo
Moon enters Libra 4:16 pm
Incense: Magnolia

◐ Sunday
Paul Bunyan Day
Waxing Moon
Second Quarter 4:16 am
Color: Amber

Moon Sign: Libra
Incense: Almond

June

29 Monday

Haro Wine Battle (Spain)
Waxing Moon
Moon phase: Second Quarter
Color: Ivory

Moon Sign: Libra
Moon enters Scorpio 6:48 pm
Incense: Hyssop

30 Tuesday

The Burning of the Three Firs (French)
Waxing Moon
Moon phase: Second Quarter
Color: Gray

Moon Sign: Scorpio
Incense: Ylang-ylang

June Birthstones

Who comes with summer to this earth,
And owes to June her hour of birth,
With ring of Agate on her hand,
Can health, wealth, and long life command.

Modern: Moonstone or Pearl
Zodiac (Gemini): Agate

July

1 Wednesday
Canada Day
Waxing Moon
Moon phase: Second Quarter
Color: Brown

Moon Sign: Scorpio
Moon enters Sagittarius 9:21 pm
Incense: Marjoram

2 Thursday
World UFO Day
Waxing Moon
Moon phase: Second Quarter
Color: Green

Moon Sign: Sagittarius
Incense: Balsam

3 Friday
Dog Days of Summer begin
Waxing Moon
Moon phase: Second Quarter
Color: Purple

Moon Sign: Sagittarius
Incense: Violet

4 Saturday
Independence Day
Waxing Moon
Moon phase: Second Quarter
Color: Blue

Moon Sign: Sagittarius
Moon enters Capricorn 12:48 am
Incense: Pine

Sunday
Tynwald Day (Manx)
Waxing Moon
Full Moon 12:44 am
Color: Gold

Moon Sign: Capricorn
Incense: Juniper

6 Monday
San Fermín begins (Spanish)
Waning Moon
Moon phase: Third Quarter
Color: Silver

Moon Sign: Capricorn
Moon enters Aquarius 6:08 am
Incense: Clary sage

7 Tuesday
Star Festival (Japanese)
Waning Moon
Moon phase: Third Quarter
Color: Black

Moon Sign: Aquarius
Incense: Cinnamon

July

8 **Wednesday**
Feast of St. Sunniva
Waning Moon
Moon phase: Third Quarter
Color: Yellow

Moon Sign: Aquarius
Moon enters Pisces 2:13 pm
Incense: Honeysuckle

9 **Thursday**
Battle of Sempach Day (Swiss)
Waning Moon
Moon phase: Third Quarter
Color: Purple

Moon Sign: Pisces
Incense: Apricot

10 **Friday**
Nicola Tesla Day
Waning Moon
Moon phase: Third Quarter
Color: Pink

Moon Sign: Pisces
Incense: Thyme

11 **Saturday**
Mongolian Naadam Festival (ends July 13)
Waning Moon
Moon phase: Third Quarter
Color: Indigo

Moon Sign: Pisces
Moon enters Aries 1:06 am
Incense: Sage

☽ **Sunday**
Malala Day
Waning Moon
Fourth Quarter 7:29 pm
Color: Yellow

Moon Sign: Aries
Incense: Hyacinth

13 **Monday**
Feast of St. Mildrith
Waning Moon
Moon phase: Fourth Quarter
Color: Lavender

Moon Sign: Aries
Moon enters Taurus 1:34 pm
Incense: Lily

14 **Tuesday**
Bastille Day (French)
Waning Moon
Moon phase: Fourth Quarter
Color: Scarlet

Moon Sign: Taurus
Incense: Bayberry

July

15 Wednesday

St. Swithin's Day
Waning Moon
Moon phase: Fourth Quarter
Color: White

Moon Sign: Taurus
Incense: Lilac

16 Thursday

Fiesta de la Tirana (Chilean)
Waning Moon
Moon phase: Fourth Quarter
Color: Crimson

Moon Sign: Taurus
Moon enters Gemini 1:19 am
Incense: Mulberry

17 Friday

Gion Festival first Yamaboko parade (Japanese)
Waning Moon
Moon phase: Fourth Quarter
Color: Coral

Moon Sign: Gemini
Incense: Yarrow

18 Saturday

Nelson Mandela International Day
Waning Moon
Moon phase: Fourth Quarter
Color: Gray

Moon Sign: Gemini
Moon enters Cancer 10:24 am
Incense: Ivy

19 Sunday

Flitch Day (English)
Waning Moon
Moon phase: Fourth Quarter
Color: Amber

Moon Sign: Cancer
Incense: Frankincense

☽ Monday

Binding of Wreaths (Lithuanian)
Waning Moon
New Moon 1:33 pm
Color: White

Moon Sign: Cancer
Moon enters Leo 4:16 pm
Incense: Narcissus

21 Tuesday

National Day (Belgian)
Waxing Moon
Moon phase: First Quarter
Color: Maroon

Moon Sign: Leo
Incense: Cedar

July

22 Wednesday
St. Mary Magdalene's Day
Waxing Moon
Moon phase: First Quarter
Color: Yellow

Moon Sign: Leo
Moon enters Virgo 7:40 pm
Sun enters Leo 4:37 am
Incense: Bay laurel

23 Thursday
Mysteries of St. Cristina (Italian)
Waxing Moon
Moon phase: First Quarter
Color: Turquoise

Moon Sign: Virgo
Incense: Myrrh

24 Friday
Gion Festival second Yamaboko parade (Japanese)
Waxing Moon
Moon phase: First Quarter
Color: Rose

Moon Sign: Virgo
Moon enters Libra 9:54 pm
Incense: Orchid

25 Saturday
Illapa Festival (Incan)
Waxing Moon
Moon phase: First Quarter
Color: Brown

Moon Sign: Libra
Incense: Sandalwood

26 Sunday
St. Anne's Day
Waxing Moon
Moon phase: First Quarter
Color: Orange

Moon Sign: Libra
Incense: Almond

☾ Monday
Sleepyhead Day (Finnish)
Waxing Moon
Second Quarter 8:33 am
Color: Ivory

Moon Sign: Libra
Moon enters Scorpio 12:12 am
Incense: Clary sage

28 Tuesday
Independence Day (Peruvian)
Waxing Moon
Moon phase: Second Quarter
Color: Gray

Moon Sign: Scorpio
Incense: Bayberry

July

29 Wednesday
St. Olaf Festival (Faroese)
Waxing Moon
Moon phase: Second Quarter
Color: Topaz

Moon Sign: Scorpio
Moon enters Sagittarius 3:25 am
Incense: Marjoram

30 Thursday
Micman Festival of St. Ann
Waxing Moon
Moon phase: Second Quarter
Color: White

Moon Sign: Sagittarius
Incense: Clove

31 Friday
Feast of St. Ignatius
Waxing Moon
Moon phase: Second Quarter
Color: Pink

Moon Sign: Sagittarius
Moon enters Capricorn 7:58 am
Incense: Vanilla

July Birthstones

The glowing Ruby shall adorn
Those who in warm July are born;
Then will they be exempt and free
From love's doubt, and anxiety.

Modern: Ruby
Zodiac (Cancer): Emerald

August

1 Saturday
Lammas
Waxing Moon
Moon phase: Second Quarter
Color: Blue

Moon Sign: Capricorn
Incense: Rue

---

2 Sunday
Porcingula (Pecos)
Waxing Moon
Moon phase: Second Quarter
Color: Amber

Moon Sign: Capricorn
Moon enters Aquarius 2:11 pm
Incense: Heliotrope

Monday
Flag Day (Venezuelan)
Waxing Moon
Full Moon 11:59 am
Color: Gray

Moon Sign: Aquarius
Incense: Rosemary

---

4 Tuesday
Constitution Day (Cook Islands)
Waning Moon
Moon phase: Third Quarter
Color: White

Moon Sign: Aquarius
Moon enters Pisces 10:28 pm
Incense: Basil

---

5 Wednesday
Carnival of Bogotá
Waning Moon
Moon phase: Third Quarter
Color: Yellow

Moon Sign: Pisces
Incense: Lavender

---

6 Thursday
Hiroshima Peace Memorial Ceremony
Waning Moon
Moon phase: Third Quarter
Color: Turquoise

Moon Sign: Pisces
Incense: Apricot

---

7 Friday
Republic Day (Ivorian)
Waning Moon
Moon phase: Third Quarter
Color: Purple

Moon Sign: Pisces
Moon enters Aries 9:05 am
Incense: Violet

August

8 Saturday

Farmers' Day (Tanzanian)
Waning Moon
Moon phase: Third Quarter
Color: Black

Moon Sign: Aries
Incense: Patchouli

---

9 Sunday

Nagasaki Peace Memorial Ceremony
Waning Moon
Moon phase: Third Quarter
Color: Orange

Moon Sign: Aries
Moon enters Taurus 9:28 pm
Incense: Marigold

---

10 Monday

Puck Fair (ends Aug. 12; Irish)
Waning Moon
Moon phase: Third Quarter
Color: Silver

Moon Sign: Taurus
Incense: Lily

◖ Tuesday

Mountain Day (Japanese)
Waning Moon
Fourth Quarter 12:45 pm
Color: Red

Moon Sign: Taurus
Incense: Geranium

---

12 Wednesday

World Elephant Day
Waning Moon
Moon phase: Fourth Quarter
Color: Brown

Moon Sign: Taurus
Moon enters Gemini 9:46 am
Incense: Lilac

---

13 Thursday

Women's Day (Tunisian)
Waning Moon
Moon phase: Fourth Quarter
Color: Green

Moon Sign: Gemini
Incense: Carnation

---

14 Friday

Independence Day (Pakistani)
Waning Moon
Moon phase: Fourth Quarter
Color: Coral

Moon Sign: Gemini
Moon enters Cancer 7:35 pm
Incense: Rose

August

15 Saturday
Bon Festival (Japanese)
Waning Moon
Moon phase: Fourth Quarter
Color: Indigo

Moon Sign: Cancer
Incense: Magnolia

---

16 Sunday
Xicolatada (French)
Waning Moon
Moon phase: Fourth Quarter
Color: Amber

Moon Sign: Cancer
Incense: Juniper

---

17 Monday
Black Cat Appreciation Day
Waning Moon
Moon phase: Fourth Quarter
Color: Lavender

Moon Sign: Cancer
Moon enters Leo 1:38 am
Incense: Neroli

Tuesday
St. Helen's Day
Waning Moon
New Moon 10:42 pm
Color: Gray

Moon Sign: Leo
Incense: Cedar

---

19 Wednesday
Vinalia Rustica (Roman)
Waxing Moon
Moon phase: First Quarter
Color: White

Moon Sign: Leo
Moon enters Virgo 4:20 am
Incense: Honeysuckle

---

20 Thursday
Islamic New Year (begins at sundown on Aug. 19)
Waxing Moon
Moon phase: First Quarter
Color: Crimson

Moon Sign: Virgo
Incense: Myrrh

---

21 Friday
Consualia (Roman)
Waxing Moon
Moon phase: First Quarter
Color: Pink

Moon Sign: Virgo
Moon enters Libra 5:16 am
Incense: Mint

August

♍

22 Saturday
Feast of the Queenship of Mary (English)
Waxing Moon
Moon phase: First Quarter
Color: Brown

Moon Sign: Libra
Sun enters Virgo 11:45 am
Incense: Sandalwood

23 Sunday
National Day (Romanian)
Waxing Moon
Moon phase: First Quarter
Color: Yellow

Moon Sign: Libra
Moon enters Scorpio 6:16 am
Incense: Frankincense

24 Monday
St. Bartholomew's Day
Waxing Moon
Moon phase: First Quarter
Color: Ivory

Moon Sign: Scorpio
Incense: Hyssop

☾ **Tuesday**
Qixi Festival (Chinese)
Waxing Moon
Second Quarter 1:58 pm
Color: Scarlet

Moon Sign: Scorpio
Moon enters Sagittarius 8:49 am
Incense: Ylang-ylang

26 Wednesday
Heroes' Day (Namibian)
Waxing Moon
Moon phase: Second Quarter
Color: Topaz

Moon Sign: Sagittarius
Incense: Bay laurel

27 Thursday
Independence Day (Moldovan)
Waxing Moon
Moon phase: Second Quarter
Color: Turquoise

Moon Sign: Sagittarius
Moon enters Capricorn 1:37 pm
Incense: Balsam

28 Friday
St. Augustine's Day
Waxing Moon
Moon phase: Second Quarter
Color: Rose

Moon Sign: Capricorn
Incense: Alder

August

29 Saturday
St. John's Beheading
Waxing Moon
Moon phase: Second Quarter
Color: Black

Moon Sign: Capricorn
Moon enters Aquarius 8:37 pm
Incense: Pine

---

30 Sunday
St. Rose of Lima Day (Peruvian)
Waxing Moon
Moon phase: Second Quarter
Color: Gold

Moon Sign: Aquarius
Incense: Eucalyptus

---

31 Monday
La Tomatina (Valencian)
Waxing Moon
Moon phase: Second Quarter
Color: Silver

Moon Sign: Aquarius
Incense: Clary sage

August Birthstones

Wear Sardonyx, or for thee
No conjugal felicity;
The August-born without this stone,
'Tis said, must live unloved, and lone.

Modern: Peridot
Zodiac (Leo): Onyx

September

1 Tuesday
Wattle Day (Australian)
Waxing Moon
Moon phase: Second Quarter
Color: Black

Moon Sign: Aquarius
Moon enters Pisces 5:34 am
Incense: Ginger

☺ Wednesday
Ghost Festival (Chinese)
Waxing Moon
Full Moon 1:22 am
Color: Yellow

Moon Sign: Pisces
Incense: Lilac

3 Thursday
National Feast of San Marino
Waning Moon
Moon phase: Third Quarter
Color: Purple

Moon Sign: Pisces
Moon enters Aries 4:22 pm
Incense: Clove

4 Friday
Feast of St. Rosalia
Waning Moon
Moon phase: Third Quarter
Color: White

Moon Sign: Aries
Incense: Yarrow

5 Saturday
International Day of Charity
Waning Moon
Moon phase: Third Quarter
Color: Brown

Moon Sign: Aries
Incense: Sage

6 Sunday
Unification Day (Bulgaria)
Waning Moon
Moon phase: Third Quarter
Color: Amber

Moon Sign: Aries
Moon enters Taurus 4:43 am
Incense: Hyacinth

7 Monday
Labor Day • Labour Day (Canadian)
Waning Moon
Moon phase: Third Quarter
Color: White

Moon Sign: Taurus
Incense: Narcissus

September

8 Tuesday
International Literacy Day
Waning Moon
Moon phase: Third Quarter
Color: Scarlet

Moon Sign: Taurus
Moon enters Gemini 5:28 pm
Incense: Cinnamon

9 Wednesday
Remembrance for Herman the Cheruscan (Asatru)
Waning Moon
Moon phase: Third Quarter
Color: Topaz

Moon Sign: Gemini
Incense: Marjoram

◑ Thursday
National Day (Belizean)
Waning Moon
Fourth Quarter 5:26 am
Color: Green

Moon Sign: Gemini
Incense: Jasmine

11 Friday
Coptic New Year
Waning Moon
Moon phase: Fourth Quarter
Color: Purple

Moon Sign: Gemini
Moon enters Cancer 4:23 am
Incense: Rose

12 Saturday
Mindfulness Day
Waning Moon
Moon phase: Fourth Quarter
Color: Gray

Moon Sign: Cancer
Incense: Patchouli

13 Sunday
Grandparents' Day
Waning Moon
Moon phase: Fourth Quarter
Color: Yellow

Moon Sign: Cancer
Moon enters Leo 11:32 am
Incense: Marigold

14 Monday
Holy Cross Day
Waning Moon
Moon phase: Fourth Quarter
Color: Ivory

Moon Sign: Leo
Incense: Lily

September

15 Tuesday
International Day of Democracy
Waning Moon
Moon phase: Fourth Quarter
Color: Red

Moon Sign: Leo
Moon enters Virgo 2:37 pm
Incense: Basil

16 Wednesday
Independence Day (Mexican)
Waning Moon
Moon phase: Fourth Quarter
Color: White

Moon Sign: Virgo
Incense: Honeysuckle

Thursday
Teachers' Day (Honduran)
Waning Moon
New Moon 7:00 am
Color: Turquoise

Moon Sign: Virgo
Moon enters Libra 2:56 pm
Incense: Clove

18 Friday
World Water Monitoring Day
Waxing Moon
Moon phase: First Quarter
Color: Rose

Moon Sign: Libra
Incense: Vanilla

19 Saturday
Rosh Hashanah (begins at sundown on Sept. 18)
Waxing Moon
Moon phase: First Quarter
Color: Blue

Moon Sign: Libra
Moon enters Scorpio 2:33 pm
Incense: Ivy

20 Sunday
St. Eustace's Day
Waxing Moon
Moon phase: First Quarter
Color: Orange

Moon Sign: Scorpio
Incense: Almond

21 Monday
UN International Day of Peace
Waxing Moon
Moon phase: First Quarter
Color: Silver

Moon Sign: Scorpio
Moon enters Sagittarius 3:32 pm
Incense: Rosemary

22 Tuesday
Mabon • Fall Equinox
Waxing Moon
Moon phase: First Quarter
Color: Maroon

Moon Sign: Sagittarius
Sun enters Libra 9:31 am
Incense: Cedar

☽ Wednesday
Feast of St. Padre Pio
Waxing Moon
Second Quarter 9:55 pm
Color: Yellow

Moon Sign: Sagittarius
Moon enters Capricorn 7:16 pm
Incense: Lavender

---

24 Thursday
Schwenkenfelder Thanksgiving (German-American)
Waxing Moon
Moon phase: Second Quarter
Color: Crimson

Moon Sign: Capricorn
Incense: Mulberry

---

25 Friday
Doll Memorial Service (Japanese)
Waxing Moon
Moon phase: Second Quarter
Color: Pink

Moon Sign: Capricorn
Incense: Orchid

---

26 Saturday
Feast of Santa Justina (Mexican)
Waxing Moon
Moon phase: Second Quarter
Color: Indigo

Moon Sign: Capricorn
Moon enters Aquarius 2:08 am
Incense: Sandalwood

---

27 Sunday
Meskel (Ethiopian and Eritrean)
Waxing Moon
Moon phase: Second Quarter
Color: Gold

Moon Sign: Aquarius
Incense: Juniper

---

28 Monday
Yom Kippur (begins at sundown on Sept. 27)
Waxing Moon
Moon phase: Second Quarter
Color: Gray

Moon Sign: Aquarius
Moon enters Pisces 11:34 am
Incense: Hyssop

September

29 Tuesday

Michaelmas
Waxing Moon
Moon phase: Second Quarter
Color: Scarlet

Moon Sign: Pisces
Incense: Bayberry

30 Wednesday

St. Jerome's Day
Waxing Moon
Moon phase: Second Quarter
Color: Brown

Moon Sign: Pisces
Moon enters Aries 10:47 pm
Incense: Bay laurel

September Birthstones

A maiden born when autumn leaves
Are rustling in September's breeze,
A Sapphire on her brow should bind;
'Twill cure diseases of the mind.

Modern: Sapphire
Zodiac (Virgo): Carnelian

October

Thursday

Mid-Autumn Festival (Chinese)
Waxing Moon
Full Moon 5:05 pm
Color: Green

Moon Sign: Aries
Incense: Apricot

---

2 Friday

Gandhi's birthday
Waning Moon
Moon phase: Third Quarter
Color: Coral

Moon Sign: Aries
Incense: Cypress

---

3 Saturday

Sukkot begins (at sundown on Oct. 2)
Waning Moon
Moon phase: Third Quarter
Color: Blue

Moon Sign: Aries
Moon enters Taurus 11:12 am
Incense: Magnolia

---

4 Sunday

St. Francis's Day
Waning Moon
Moon phase: Third Quarter
Color: Yellow

Moon Sign: Taurus
Incense: Frankincense

---

5 Monday

Republic Day (Portuguese)
Waning Moon
Moon phase: Third Quarter
Color: Ivory

Moon Sign: Taurus
Incense: Neroli

---

6 Tuesday

German-American Day
Waning Moon
Moon phase: Third Quarter
Color: Gray

Moon Sign: Taurus
Moon enters Gemini 12:03 am
Incense: Cinnamon

---

7 Wednesday

Nagasaki Kunchi Festival (ends Oct. 9)
Waning Moon
Moon phase: Third Quarter
Color: Yellow

Moon Sign: Gemini
Incense: Marjoram

October

8 **Thursday**
Arbor Day (Namibian)
Waning Moon
Moon phase: Third Quarter
Color: Purple

Moon Sign: Gemini
Moon enters Cancer 11:45 am
Incense: Balsam

○ **Friday**
Sukkot ends
Waning Moon
Fourth Quarter 8:40 pm
Color: Rose

Moon Sign: Cancer
Incense: Violet

10 **Saturday**
Finnish Literature Day
Waning Moon
Moon phase: Fourth Quarter
Color: Indigo

Moon Sign: Cancer
Moon enters Leo 8:24 pm
Incense: Pine

11 **Sunday**
Meditrinalia (Roman)
Waning Moon
Moon phase: Fourth Quarter
Color: Orange

Moon Sign: Leo
Incense: Hyacinth

12 **Monday**
Thanksgiving Day (Canadian) • Indigenous Peoples' Day
Waning Moon
Moon phase: Fourth Quarter
Color: Lavender

Moon Sign: Leo
Incense: Clary sage

13 **Tuesday**
Fontinalia (Roman)
Waning Moon
Moon phase: Fourth Quarter
Color: Red

Moon Sign: Leo
Moon enters Virgo 12:56 am
Incense: Geranium

14 **Wednesday**
National Education Day (Polish)
Waning Moon
Moon phase: Fourth Quarter
Color: White

Moon Sign: Virgo
Incense: Lilac

October

15 Thursday
The October Horse (Roman)
Waning Moon
Moon phase: Fourth Quarter
Color: Turquoise

Moon Sign: Virgo
Moon enters Libra 1:54 am
Incense: Nutmeg

Friday
The Lion Sermon (British)
Waning Moon
New Moon 3:31 pm
Color: Pink

Moon Sign: Libra
Incense: Alder

17 Saturday
Dessalines Day (Haitian)
Waxing Moon
Moon phase: First Quarter
Color: Black

Moon Sign: Libra
Moon enters Scorpio 1:05 am
Incense: Sage

18 Sunday
Feast of St. Luke
Waxing Moon
Moon phase: First Quarter
Color: Yellow

Moon Sign: Scorpio
Incense: Almond

19 Monday
Mother Teresa Day (Albanian)
Waxing Moon
Moon phase: First Quarter
Color: White

Moon Sign: Scorpio
Moon enters Sagittarius 12:43 am
Incense: Narcissus

20 Tuesday
Feast of St. Acca
Waxing Moon
Moon phase: First Quarter
Color: Black

Moon Sign: Sagittarius
Incense: Ylang-ylang

21 Wednesday
Apple Day (United Kingdom)
Waxing Moon
Moon phase: First Quarter
Color: Topaz

Moon Sign: Sagittarius
Moon enters Capricorn 2:44 am
Incense: Honeysuckle

October

22 Thursday

Jidai Festival (Japanese)
Waxing Moon
Moon phase: First Quarter
Color: Purple

Moon Sign: Capricorn
Sun enters Scorpio 7:00 pm
Incense: Mulberry

◑ Friday

Revolution Day (Hungarian)
Waxing Moon
Second Quarter 9:23 am
Color: White

Moon Sign: Capricorn
Moon enters Aquarius 8:17 am
Incense: Mint

24 Saturday

United Nations Day
Waxing Moon
Moon phase: Second Quarter
Color: Gray

Moon Sign: Aquarius
Incense: Rue

25 Sunday

St. Crispin's Day
Waxing Moon
Moon phase: Second Quarter
Color: Gold

Moon Sign: Aquarius
Moon enters Pisces 5:18 pm
Incense: Juniper

26 Monday

Death of Alfred the Great
Waxing Moon
Moon phase: Second Quarter
Color: Silver

Moon Sign: Pisces
Incense: Rosemary

27 Tuesday

Feast of St. Abbán
Waxing Moon
Moon phase: Second Quarter
Color: Scarlet

Moon Sign: Pisces
Incense: Ginger

28 Wednesday

Ohi Day (Greek)
Waxing Moon
Moon phase: Second Quarter
Color: White

Moon Sign: Pisces
Moon enters Aries 4:45 am
Incense: Bay laurel

October

29 Thursday
National Cat Day
Waxing Moon
Moon phase: Second Quarter
Color: Crimson

Moon Sign: Aries
Incense: Carnation

---

30 Friday
John Adams's birthday
Waxing Moon
Moon phase: Second Quarter
Color: Purple

Moon Sign: Aries
Moon enters Taurus 5:19 pm
Incense: Yarrow

Saturday
Halloween • Samhain
Waxing Moon
Full Moon 10:49 am
Color: Brown

Moon Sign: Taurus
Incense: Patchouli

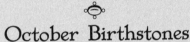

October Birthstones

October's child is born for woe,
And life's vicissitudes must know;
But lay an Opal on her breast,
And hope will lull those foes to rest.

Modern: Opal or Tourmaline
Zodiac (Libra): Peridot

November

1 Sunday
All Saints' Day • Día de los Muertos
Waning Moon
Moon phase: Third Quarter
Color: Orange

Moon Sign: Taurus
Incense: Eucalyptus
Daylight Saving Time ends at 2 am

2 Monday
All Souls' Day
Waning Moon
Moon phase: Third Quarter
Color: White

Moon Sign: Taurus
Moon enters Gemini 5:00 am
Incense: Lily

3 Tuesday
Election Day (general)
Waning Moon
Moon phase: Third Quarter
Color: Black

Moon Sign: Gemini
Incense: Basil

4 Wednesday
Mischief Night (British)
Waning Moon
Moon phase: Third Quarter
Color: Yellow

Moon Sign: Gemini
Moon enters Cancer 4:45 pm
Incense: Lavender

5 Thursday
Guy Fawkes Night (British)
Waning Moon
Moon phase: Third Quarter
Color: Turquoise

Moon Sign: Cancer
Incense: Myrrh

6 Friday
St. Leonard's Ride (German)
Waning Moon
Moon phase: Third Quarter
Color: Pink

Moon Sign: Cancer
Incense: Orchid

7 Saturday
Feast of St. Willibrord
Waning Moon
Moon phase: Third Quarter
Color: Blue

Moon Sign: Cancer
Moon enters Leo 2:18 pm
Incense: Sandalwood

November

◐ **Sunday**
World Urbanism Day
Waning Moon
Fourth Quarter 8:46 am
Color: Amber

Moon Sign: Leo
Incense: Heliotrope

---

9 Monday
Fateful Day (German)
Waning Moon
Moon phase: Fourth Quarter
Color: Silver

Moon Sign: Leo
Moon enters Virgo 8:30 am
Incense: Hyssop

---

10 Tuesday
Martin Luther's Birthday
Waning Moon
Moon phase: Fourth Quarter
Color: Maroon

Moon Sign: Virgo
Incense: Cedar

---

11 Wednesday
Veterans Day • Remembrance Day (Canadian)
Waning Moon
Moon phase: Fourth Quarter
Color: Brown

Moon Sign: Virgo
Moon enters Libra 11:09 am
Incense: Marjoram

---

12 Thursday
Feast Day of San Diego (Tesuque Puebloan)
Waning Moon
Moon phase: Fourth Quarter
Color: Crimson

Moon Sign: Libra
Incense: Clove

---

13 Friday
Festival of Jupiter
Waning Moon
Moon phase: Fourth Quarter
Color: White

Moon Sign: Libra
Moon enters Scorpio 11:19 am
Incense: Rose

---

14 Saturday
Diwali
Waning Moon
Moon phase: Fourth Quarter
Color: Black

Moon Sign: Scorpio
Incense: Magnolia

November

☽ **Sunday**
Seven-Five-Three Festival (Japanese)
Waning Moon
New Moon 12:07 am
Color: Gold

Moon Sign: Scorpio
Moon enters Sagittarius 10:47 am
Incense: Marigold

---

16 Monday
St. Margaret of Scotland's Day
Waxing Moon
Moon phase: First Quarter
Color: Gray

Moon Sign: Sagttarius
Incense: Narcissus

---

17 Tuesday
Queen Elizabeth's Ascension Day
Waxing Moon
Moon phase: First Quarter
Color: Red

Moon Sign: Sagittarius
Moon Capricorn 11:35 am
Incense: Ylang-ylang

---

18 Wednesday
Independence Day (Moroccan)
Waxing Moon
Moon phase: First Quarter
Color: Topaz

Moon Sign: Capricorn
Incense: Lilac

---

19 Thursday
Garifuna Settlement Day (Belizean)
Waxing Moon
Moon phase: First Quarter
Color: Purple

Moon Sign: Capricorn
Moon enters Aquarius 3:25 pm
Incense: Jasmine

---

20 Friday
Native American Heritage Day
Waxing Moon
Moon phase: First Quarter
Color: Rose

Moon Sign: Aquarius
Incense: Cypress

◑ **Saturday**
National Adoption Day
Waxing Moon
Second Quarter 11:45 pm
Color: Brown

Moon Sign: Aquarius
Moon enters Pisces 11:06 pm
Sun enters Sagittarius 3:40 pm
Incense: Rue

November

22 Sunday
St. Cecilia's Day
Waxing Moon
Moon phase: Second Quarter
Color: Orange

Moon Sign: Pisces
Incense: Frankincense

23 Monday
St. Clement's Day
Waxing Moon
Moon phase: Second Quarter
Color: Lavender

Moon Sign: Pisces
Incense: Rosemary

24 Tuesday
Evolution Day
Waxing Moon
Moon phase: Second Quarter
Color: Scarlet

Moon Sign: Pisces
Moon enters Aries 10:05 am
Incense: Geranium

25 Wednesday
Feast of St. Catherine of Alexandria
Waxing Moon
Moon phase: Second Quarter
Color: White

Moon Sign: Aries
Incense: Bay laurel

26 Thursday
Thanksgiving Day (US)
Waxing Moon
Moon phase: Second Quarter
Color: Green

Moon Sign: Aries
Moon enters Taurus 10:43 pm
Incense: Nutmeg

27 Friday
Feast of St. Virgilius
Waxing Moon
Moon phase: Second Quarter
Color: Coral

Moon Sign: Taurus
Incense: Thyme

28 Saturday
Republic Day (Chadian)
Waxing Moon
Moon phase: Second Quarter
Color: Blue

Moon Sign: Taurus
Incense: Ivy

November

29 **Sunday**

William Tubman's birthday (Liberian)
Waxing Moon
Moon phase: Second Quarter
Color: Yellow

Moon Sign: Taurus
Moon enters Gemini 11:16 am
Incense: Almond

 Monday

St. Andrew's Day (Scottish)
Waxing Moon
Full Moon 4:30 am
Color: Ivory

Moon Sign: Gemini
Incense: Neroli

November Birthstones

Who first come to this world below,
With drear November's fog, and snow,
Should prize the Topaz's amber hue,
Emblem of friends, and lovers true.

Modern: Topaz or Citrine
Zodiac (Scorpio): Beryl

December

1 Tuesday
Feast for Death of Aleister Crowley (Thelemic)
Waning Moon
Moon phase: Third Quarter
Color: Black

Moon Sign: Gemini
Moon enters Cancer 10:33 pm
Incense: Ginger

2 Wednesday
Republic Day (Laotian)
Waning Moon
Moon phase: Third Quarter
Color: Yellow

Moon Sign: Cancer
Incense: Lavender

3 Thursday
St. Francis Xavier's Day
Waning Moon
Moon phase: Third Quarter
Color: White

Moon Sign: Cancer
Incense: Apricot

4 Friday
Feasts of Shango and St. Barbara
Waning Moon
Moon phase: Third Quarter
Color: Purple

Moon Sign: Cancer
Moon enters Leo 7:53 am
Incense: Alder

5 Saturday
Krampus Night (European)
Waning Moon
Moon phase: Third Quarter
Color: Gray

Moon Sign: Leo
Incense: Sage

6 Sunday
St. Nicholas's Day
Waning Moon
Moon phase: Third Quarter
Color: Orange

Moon Sign: Leo
Moon enters Virgo 2:46 pm
Incense: Marigold

◐ Monday
Burning the Devil (Guatemalan)
Waning Moon
Fourth Quarter 7:37 pm
Color: Silver

Moon Sign: Virgo
Incense: Clary sage

December

8 Tuesday
Bodhi Day (Japanese)
Waning Moon
Moon phase: Fourth Quarter
Color: Scarlet

Moon Sign: Virgo
Moon enters Libra 7:01 pm
Incense: Bayberry

9 Wednesday
Anna's Day (Sweden)
Waning Moon
Moon phase: Fourth Quarter
Color: White

Moon Sign: Libra
Incense: Honeysuckle

10 Thursday
Alfred Nobel Day
Waning Moon
Moon phase: Fourth Quarter
Color: Crimson

Moon Sign: Libra
Moon enters Scorpio 8:59 pm
Incense: Myrrh

11 Friday
Hanukkah begins (at sundown on Dec. 10)
Waning Moon
Moon phase: Fourth Quarter
Color: Coral

Moon Sign: Scorpio
Incense: Vanilla

12 Saturday
Fiesta of Our Lady of Guadalupe (Mexican)
Waning Moon
Moon phase: Fourth Quarter
Color: Indigo

Moon Sign: Scorpio
Moon enters Sagittarius 9:39 pm
Incense: Pine

13 Sunday
St. Lucy's Day (Scandinavian and Italian)
Waning Moon
Moon phase: Fourth Quarter
Color: Gold

Moon Sign: Sagittarius
Incense: Heliotrope

☽ Monday
Forty-Seven Ronin Memorial (Japanese)
Waning Moon
New Moon 11:17 am
Color: White

Moon Sign: Sagittarius
Moon enters Capricorn 10:35 pm
Incense: Lily

December

15 Tuesday
Consualia (Roman)
Waxing Moon
Moon phase: First Quarter
Color: Maroon

Moon Sign: Capricorn
Incense: Cedar

---

16 Wednesday
Las Posadas begin (end Dec. 24)
Waxing Moon
Moon phase: First Quarter
Color: Brown

Moon Sign: Capricorn
Incense: Bay laurel

---

17 Thursday
Saturnalia (Roman)
Waxing Moon
Moon phase: First Quarter
Color: Turquoise

Moon Sign: Capricorn
Moon enters Aquarius 1:27 am
Incense: Clove

---

18 Friday
Hanukkah ends
Waxing Moon
Moon phase: First Quarter
Color: Rose

Moon Sign: Aquarius
Incense: Rose

---

19 Saturday
Opalia (Roman)
Waxing Moon
Moon phase: First Quarter
Color: Black

Moon Sign: Aquarius
Moon enters Pisces 7:39 am
Incense: Sandalwood

---

20 Sunday
Feast of St. Dominic of Silos
Waxing Moon
Moon phase: First Quarter
Color: Yellow

Moon Sign: Pisces
Incense: Juniper

☽ Monday
Yule • Winter Solstice
Waxing Moon
Second Quarter 6:41 pm
Color: Gray

Moon Sign: Pisces
Moon enters Aries 5:32 pm
Sun enters Capricorn 5:02 am
Incense: Hyssop

December

22 Tuesday
Feasts of SS. Chaeremon and Ischyrion
Waxing Moon
Moon phase: Second Quarter
Color: Red

Moon Sign: Aries
Incense: Ylang-ylang

---

23 Wednesday
Larentalia (Roman)
Waxing Moon
Moon phase: Second Quarter
Color: Topaz

Moon Sign: Aries
Incense: Lilac

---

24 Thursday
Christmas Eve
Waxing Moon
Moon phase: Second Quarter
Color: Purple

Moon Sign: Aries
Moon enters Taurus 5:55 am
Incense: Apricot

---

25 Friday
Christmas Day
Waxing Moon
Moon phase: Second Quarter
Color: Pink

Moon Sign: Taurus
Incense: Cypress

---

26 Saturday
Kwanzaa begins (ends Jan. 1) • Boxing Day
Waxing Moon
Moon phase: Second Quarter
Color: Blue

Moon Sign: Taurus
Moon enters Gemini 6:33 pm
Incense: Patchouli

---

27 Sunday
St. Stephen's Day
Waxing Moon
Moon phase: Second Quarter
Color: Gold

Moon Sign: Gemini
Incense: Almond

---

28 Monday
Feast of the Holy Innocents
Waxing Moon
Moon phase: Second Quarter
Color: Ivory

Moon Sign: Gemini
Incense: Neroli

December

 Tuesday
Feast of St. Thomas à Becket
Waxing Moon
Full Moon 10:28 pm
Color: Gray

Moon Sign: Gemini
Moon enters Cancer 5:28 am
Incense: Cinnamon

---

30 Wednesday
Republic Day (Madagascan)
Waning Moon
Moon phase: Third Quarter
Color: Yellow

Moon Sign: Cancer
Incense: Marjoram

---

31 Thursday
New Year's Eve
Waning Moon
Moon phase: Third Quarter
Color: White

Moon Sign: Cancer
Moon enters Leo 1:58 pm
Incense: Balsam

December Birthstones

If cold December gives you birth,
The month of snow, and ice, and mirth,
Place in your hand a Turquoise blue;
Success will bless whate'er you do.

Modern: Turquoise or Blue Topaz
Zodiac (Sagittarius): Topaz

Fire Magic

Transportation Mojo

Blake Octavian Blair

We all have to go from point A to point B, the majority of us daily. Most of us would like to use our magickal knowledge and skill to mojo up our transportation experience a bit—add a bit of calm, surround ourselves with an ethereal level of protection, and generally smooth out our commute from location to location. In other words, we want to employ a bit of transportation mojo. There are a variety of ways to do this, so let's take a look at a few ways to go about deploying our magickal power before we go dig into our magickal supply cupboards.

"Altared" Vehicles

Among magickal folk, a popular way to begin magickally jazzing up our transportation is to create a car altar. If you have a car of your own, the dashboard seems to just be sitting there, begging for a little bit of enchantment! Dashboard car altars range from simple to elaborate. The goal of most dashboard altars is to invoke protection and calm during travel. With those goals in mind, a good place to begin building your altar is by selecting an image of a spirit, power animal, or deity you work with that embodies those qualities. In India, for example, it is commonplace to have a statue of the elephant god Ganesha on the dashboard. Ganesha has become a popular choice due to his lovable nature and associations with luck, prosperity, and removing obstacles. It's not a bad combination of qualities to have in your favor while traveling! I've worked with Ganesha for years, and he was my choice when it came to deciding who to put on my dashboard. In Thailand, for similar reasons, almost any taxicab that you hail will have a beautiful and often ornate altar to the Buddha on the dash. Catholics will often have a statue of Virgin Mary on the dash, and although they may not call it travel magick, under our definitions it certainly is!

One of my grove-mates has a very creative approach to her dashboard altar. In her travels she does her best to connect with the seasons and nature. After all, we do see it out the windshield right before our very eyes as we are zipping down the road. So she rotates, changes, and spruces up her dashboard with the change of the seasons. Each season she finds seasonally thematical and fun items. For example, summertime brings a stylish and fun little pink flamingo to her dashboard as a travel companion! Autumn may bring a small icon of a pumpkin and so on.

A shamanic approach is to feature a personal totem or power animal in your car altar. If you have such strong guardians in your life, it only makes sense to petition them during your travels. A small figurine or a printed or laminated image of your animal can be the central feature that you build around. In addition to the animal, often included are many other objects from nature that lend their spirit for protection and guidance. Examples of popular objects are rocks found from places you have a connection with,

found feathers or bones, or twigs from branches of trees with the desired associations. A note on found feathers: while feathers are wonderful inclusions for travel magick due to their obvious association with the smooth air travel of their original bearers, many feathers are protected and illegal to possess. Research a type of feather before claiming it as yours to see if it's within the guidelines of those permissible to obtain and possess.

Rearview Magick

Hanging charms, amulets, and talismans from the rearview mirror is a popular method of adding a bit of car mojo. If you go this route, I always recommend something very simple, conservative in size, so as to limit it causing a distraction or obscuring your view while driving. For this very reason, many states have actually banned hanging objects from the rearview mirror, so check your local laws before hanging anything. However, simple charms, such as a crystal on a string or a very small picture of a deity with a cord threaded through it, can work well hanging from the mirror. Very small mojo and medicine bags work well hung from the mirror as well. Later on we'll discuss some simple ingredients for such a bag. Some choose to hang prayer beads or rosaries from the rearview mirror. Some consider this a bit sacrilegious, while other people find it the perfect charm.

A talisman I often see hung from rear view mirrors that I do not understand is the Native American dreamcatcher. All my friends who are of Native American heritage are also confused about why someone would want to hang a sleep talisman on their rearview mirror while driving. It seems a bit, shall we say, counterintuitive to the goals of safe travel! My point being, think through the objects you are considering including in your transportation mojo. Make sure they're effective for your goals.

Mojo Undercover

Some people desire less visible tactics that allow for clandestine mojo. There are plenty of options to accomplish this, and luckily an automobile provides many wonderful hiding spots! From the glove box, to seat back pockets, to under the seats, to armrest compartments, there are plenty of places to stash some magickal goodness out of sight but effectively in the vehicle. This can be as easy as programming a small rock or crystal and placing it in the trunk or securely under a seat, or it might be slightly more involved, like the cre-

A Little Bit of Magic

WHEN YOU'RE DEALING WITH LIMITED SPACE, YOU WANT TO GO SIMPLE BUT POWERFUL.

ation of a charm bag to put under the seat. There is really no right or wrong answer for the number of ingredients you want to put into your spell bag. However, it's interesting to note that traditionally the gris-gris style spell bags contain odd numbers of ingredients ranging from three to thirteen . . . magickal numbers indeed!

To create a simple transportation mojo bag, take a small square of fabric in a color that resonates with you for safety and protection, along with some ribbon or twine, a small quartz crystal, and a couple of the following herbs associated with safe travel: oregano, mugwort, comfrey, lavender, and mint. Lay the square of fabric out flat, and as you focus on your intent, place a small amount of each ingredient, finishing with the crystal, onto the center of the square. Then, hold your hands over it and send your energy of intent into the mound of ingredients. Draw the corners up and tie it shut with the cord. You can further affirm your intentions into the bag by cupping it in your hands and blowing your intent into it. Now place your creation discreetly inside your vehicle.

Vehicle Blessings

Another method of transportation mojo is performing a vehicle blessing. If you've never heard of this before, it's similar to what you'd think of with a home blessing only geared and scaled for a vehicle. A general blessing with the elements utilizing holy water,

smudge, incense, and recitation of prayers and intentions is performed inside and outside around the vehicle to invoke safety and protection for the vehicle and all who travel in it. You might even use a magickal oil that fits your purposes to anoint the steering wheel, tires, and more. Once the blessing is performed, the vehicle looks just like any other, carrying your clandestine magick. This also works no matter how large or small the vehicle, from skateboards and bicycles to cars and RVs. Are you also a frequent pedestrian? Anoint and bless those walking shoes! Enchant your shoelaces! Get creative—transportation mojo is for all.

Mojo Wanted: No Automobile Required

As I mentioned, perhaps you don't own an automobile. Clearly, many transportation mojo tactics are applicable whether you own an automobile, ride a bicycle, are a pedestrian, or take public transportation. Magickal knowledge has the wonderful ability to be adapted to your individual circumstances. For example, with a bicycle, you still have wheels you can anoint, albeit two instead of four. You may not have a steering wheel, but you have handlebars. Further, while it is true a bicycle has no trunk or glove compartment, you can add a bicycle bag or basket. All of a sudden, the majority of the little mojo tricks for cars are again possible!

The adventure that is public transit is an almost daily experience for big-city dwellers. Even those who find themselves mainly on foot, buses, and subway trains need not fret. Whether your key chain has a car key on it or not, it's an excellent transportation mojo opportunity. Simple crystal key chains can be bought or made and enchanted for safe travel on your key chain. Perhaps you can find a charm or talisman to slip in your key ring that connects you with a power animal or patron or matron deity. The possibilities are endless.

Those who travel via walking and public transportation generally carry a purse, briefcase, backpack, or other bag with them regularly. Guess what? Just like a bag or basket on a bicycle, your bag now becomes your surrogate "car trunk." As a magickal practitioner, I know you're already utilizing your bag to bring little bits of magick with you, so add some of the transportation mojo ideas from this article to your bag's inventory!

You also do not have to leave your shoes out of the transportation mojo party. As mentioned earlier, you can bless and anoint your walking shoes for safe travel. But you can also raise the bar even more. With magickal intent and a permanent marker, you can take the enchantment one step further. Choose or design a sigil or rune for safe travel. Then while focusing on your intent, turn that marker into a wand, and with deliberate motion draw the sigil inside the shoe where your foot will rest. Nobody will ever see it, and you'll be clandestinely mojo-ed up! You may need to periodically redraw it as it wears away from use over time; however, this is simply a chance to re-up your fabulous mojo.

Washing Up!

There's also a fabulous old Hoodoo practice called a wash. If you're unfamiliar, this is generally a liquid mixture of water and other herbal and magickal ingredients that is then applied or "washed"

onto something for a specific purpose. It's easy to formulate your own magickal wash for transportation mojo: simply consult your favorite magickal herbal and correspondence references. You'll likely find you have most of the ingredients "in house" in either your kitchen or magickal cupboards (though I think the kitchen cupboard is simply an extension of one's magickal cupboards!). However, I'm going to include an easy recipe for a basic wash that will get you on the road (pun intended)! The recipe is a guideline, so feel free to adjust quantities and substitute ingredients as needed. In a bucket full of hot water, place the following:

2 tablespoons Florida water
9 drops pine oil or 9 pine needles
1 cinnamon stick
Sprinkle of fennel

Allow ingredients to steep for about ten minutes, and then use a sponge and give your vehicle or the exterior of your shoes a wash with the mixture while envisioning a growing protective light surrounding your mode of transportation. When finished, pour the bucket of wash mixture onto the earth for transmutation of any stray energy.

· · · ☽ · · ·

While this brief overview of transportation mojo methods is simple and to the point, I hope it has your magickal muse brewing a trunkload of magickal possibilities for you. No matter your mode of transportation, may you have a safe and blessed journey along your path!

Resources

Bradley, Jude, and Cheré Dastugue Coen. *Magic's in the Bag: Creating Spellbinding Gris Gris Bags & Sachets.* Woodbury, MN: Llewellyn Publications, 2010.

Cunningham, Scott. *Cunningham's Encyclopedia of Magical Herbs.* St. Paul, MN: Llewellyn Publications, 1985.

Entropic Magic

Elizabeth Barrette

The universe balances between forces of creation and forces of destruction. *Syntropy* is a force that builds and organizes. Life and crystallization are examples of syntropy. *Entropy* is a force that breaks down and disorganizes. Decay and heat loss are examples of entropy. Think of them like winding and unwinding a clock spring. Both are needed to keep the universe in good working order. Let's explore the nature of entropy and its constructive uses, such as gardening, banishing, and recycling.

Many people shy away from working entropic magic. They may think of it as "dark" or "evil." It is neither; it's a natural force with its own rules and benefits, like any other. So entropic magic can help anyone who needs to break down or get rid of things and is willing to use magic that isn't all cute flowers and shiny stones. It probably appeals more to Hedge Witches than to ceremonialists. However, some of the most powerful banishing spells are elaborate ritualistic constructs. There's something in it for everyone.

What Is Entropy?

Entropy is a scientific process. Various laws and formulas express the tendency of systems to lose energy over time and to progress from order toward disorder. For example, if you drop a ball, it will bounce less and less until it lies still, not bounce more. If you bump a tower of stacked blocks, they will fall into a random pattern, not an organized pattern.

While these processes are often inconvenient, we rely on them for our survival. Entropy is what breaks things down so they can be reused. Without it, dead things and waste products would not decay and would soon bury the world in refuse. Things that don't break down readily—such as nuclear waste and plastic trash—cause tremendous problems in the environment precisely because they impede the natural process of entropy. We need entropy to remove things we don't want anymore and to make way for new things.

Magical Aspects of Entropy

Entropy isn't neat and pretty. It's grungy and messy. For this reason, people may avoid it or misunderstand it. That complicates the discussion of ethics in entropic magic. Death isn't evil, but because people fear it, everything associated with it seems bad or scary. However, there's nothing inherently wrong with it; death is a natural process. So working with entropy isn't unethical unto itself. You just have to follow the moral guidelines of your tradition. For instance, killing people is generally considered wrong, but working magic to help them understand death as a life event is all right.

Entropy has many magical applications. As with any field of magic, some of these are more ethical than others. When you think about breaking down a connection, the morality depends on the condition of the bond itself. Breaking someone's relationship so you can take their place would be wrong, but eroding an abusive relationship to help someone escape is very different. Generally, causing things to rot is a problem, but if you keep a compost pile or raise mushrooms, then you want to support that process of decay. Similarly, recycling takes things that are thrown away and makes something new. It lets us conserve resources, which is good.

Consider the correspondences of entropy in magic. Among deities, all tricksters and death deities count. So do individual patrons of entropic manifestations, such as Ningišzida, Mesopotamian god of growth and decay, or Cheukshin, Korean toilet goddess. Invoke tricksters for necessary destruction and death deities for times of transition. Invoke patrons when dealing with their area of influence—Ningišzida will bless your compost pile, and Cheukshin will help you find a plumber in the middle of the night.

Other correspondences can be used in spellcraft. Sunset and night are entropic times of day, readily available. The waning moon represents monthly declines, ideal for banishing and certain types of gardening. Autumn and winter are entropic times of year, good for long-term spells. All of these have syntropic counterparts. When doing cyclic magic, you want to balance them—night and day, waning and waxing Moon, fallow season and farm season, and so on.

Gardening

Gardens run on entropy in many ways. Plants break down soil to extract nutrients. Some garden systems pile up organic matter to cope with poor soil. Invertebrates keep soil and plants healthy. Many of them belong to the detritus food chain, linking the forces of life and death. Ningišzida is a natural here. Let's explore ways you can use entropic magic in your garden.

Bless your compost pile to stay healthy, break down faster, and not turn into a reeking anaerobic mess. Healthy compost requires a good working balance of "brown" things high in carbon, such as leaves or wood chips, and "green" things high in nitrogen, such as grass clippings or vegetable scraps. It can take months to turn raw materials into finished compost ready to spread on your garden.

Use entropic magic and you cut down that time. Invoke deities of decay during a waning Moon.

Similarly, hügelkultur is a gardening system that relies on making a big pile of organic matter for growing plants. It uses branches or logs as the core, then twigs and leaves, with a coating of soil. You want it to break down at "just the right speed," so do the entropic blessing under a Full Moon, the balance between waxing and waning. If you're building a new hügelkultur, do it in autumn or early winter so it has time to mature during the entropic season before spring brings new life.

You can farm the detritus food web! Grow edible mushrooms in a bed of compost or on host logs. Grow earthworms in a vermiculture bin. Use entropic magic to encourage the growth of what you want and discourage competing pests. This is one case where waxing Moon energy supports entropic magic.

Miner plants have deep roots that delve into subsoil or bedrock to extract useful minerals. In the garden, they make those nutrients more available for nearby plants. Some miners, such as comfrey, grow so big and fast you can use the "slash and drop" method—just cut them and leave them where they lie. As they decay, they'll re-

lease the minerals. Entropic magic makes it easier for these plants to break down the subsoil and encourages the cut tops to rot faster. Cut them during a waning Moon.

Banishing

Entropy also rules all forms of magic for getting rid of things. You can banish a negative entity, an unwelcome person, a bad habit, garden pests, and so on. These spells often involve a symbolic act of destruction or repulsion that shapes the energy to drive out what you don't want. Consider deities such as Zeus, who banished the Titans to the underworld; Kali, a goddess of destruction and chaos; or Hecate, crone goddess of the Dark Moon.

Elemental banishings can destroy a symbolic item in many ways. Let's say you have a picture of your bad habit. If you tear it up and let the pieces blow away, that's air magic. If you burn it and scatter the ashes at a crossroad, that's fire magic. If you make it into a paper boat and float it down a river, that's water magic. If you bury it under your compost pile, that's earth magic. But they're all elemental variations of entropic magic. Burying it in the compost pile is among the best, because compost is designed to turn waste products into something useful. It's also safe, and you're not littering. Just make sure your symbolic item is compostable.

Some types of banishing rely on breaking an object. This works best when you need to get rid of an abusive person, a bad job, a house you hate, and so on. Suppose you have a coffee cup from the bad job. Wrap it in a cloth, smash it with a hammer, and send the pieces to a landfill, which is another entropic place of power.

Other types of banishing use substances that break down or repel. Everyone knows about things like salt and charcoal. But you can get creative. Hot peppers, pepper flakes, pepper oil, and so on make great banishing components and figure in the famous Hotfoot Oil to make someone go away. Think about how entropic things work. Solvents melt things, good for dissolving connections. If you have someone acting like a stone wall in your path, mix in some comfrey powder to break down the resistance just like comfrey breaks down stones. Be careful with magic involving other people; some traditions, such as Voudoun, allow it, while others, such as Wicca, limit or prohibit it.

Re(cycling)

Entropy is half the power behind a balanced cycle. Birth, life, and growth are the syntropic side. Decline, death, and decay are the entropic side—after which comes rebirth. Neither half can function properly without the other. Without decay during autumn and winter, there would be no fertilizer to feed the new plants in spring. For this reason, entropy is an essential component for cyclic magic. Here you want figures of transformation such as Circe, a witch who used shape-shifting; Tiresias, a gender-shifter; Heqet, the Egyptian frog goddess; or Xochipilli, the Aztec god of butterflies and vegetation.

The most common cyclic magic among Pagans is lunar magic. To put both halves into a Moon spell, first banish what you don't want during the waning Moon, and then attract what you want to replace it during the waxing Moon. You can use a similar approach with night and day.

Another popular example is seasonal magic. Autumn is the time of harvest, when plants and animals are cut off to be eaten. Fields are tilled under. It's a good time to start projects that need to cure over the winter and, of course, to plant bulbs that will bloom in spring. Winter is the time of rest, the low ebb of energy when entropy is strongest. All is cold and still. Then spring comes and life renews itself. Compost gets added to gardens. Summer is the height of syntropy, when everything is warm and growing. But summer leans toward autumn, when all that growth comes to fruition and then dies. For maximum effect, you need to work magic all around that wheel, not ignore the entropic part. Seasonal magic takes a lot of commitment to work for a whole year, but it's great for big projects like farming, fertility, a college education, and so on.

Reusing items in their current form with a new application is a subtle example of entropy. Nice clothes become everyday clothes become grubbies, and when you can't wear the grubbies, you cut them down for rags. Save your cotton rags to make torches! Synthetics don't work because they melt, but cotton makes a terrific wick, and a torchlit procession to ritual is a thing to remember. An old desk can be converted to an altar table. Sand it down and repaint it with a pentacle on top. Collect stubs of candles, crayons, and other wax scraps. Melt them down to become new candles by adding wicks, or dip pine cones in the melted wax to make firestart-ers for your ritual bonfires.

A more dramatic form is recycling. It takes old things and re-processes them into something new. Plastic bottles become shoes or reusable shopping bags. Office paper becomes newspaper or toilet paper. Tires become mud mats. Glass and metal melt down to make bottles or cans again. To invoke transformative entropy in-stead of destructive entropy, use a recyclable material as your sym-bol and then recycle it. When choosing items to use in an entropic ritual, look for things made from recycled material. Among the most spectacular is silk yarn made from recycled sari silk scraps. It's great for cord magic. Recycling is a form of entropic activity that humans need to do more of.

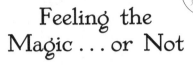

Feeling the
Magic . . . or Not

Thorn Mooney

"That was amazing! I could really feel the energy of the circle!"

"Yeah, me too! That was totally intense. It was like I could *see* the circle."

Oh no. It was happening again. The ritual had ended twenty minutes ago and we were all standing around at the potluck scooping potato salad onto plates and sharing our experiences. I was a young Witch, still finding my feet in the Craft. I'd spent the last couple of years reading books and hanging out online looking for other Pagans, and I was so excited to find out that there was a community center nearby that sometimes hosted Pagan and Wiccan events for the public. I'd already been to a few, but I could see there was a pattern developing. After the circle came the part I dreaded, when everyone would hang out and talk about their magical experiences. Even though I was attending the exact same rituals, I never felt like I had anything worthwhile to say!

"How about you, Thorn? Wasn't that amazing?"

"Um . . . yeah! Great!"

I spent a lot of time lying in my early years of exploring magic, both to other people and to myself. The truth was, I was starting to think I just wasn't cut out to be a Witch. I just never seemed to get what other people got out of ritual. I'd look around at the other faces standing in the circle with me—their eyes closed, their breathing focused and heavy, their gesticulations and *blessed be*s always so full of feeling—and I'd feel like a fraud. Witchcraft was important to me. It had changed my life, in fact, as it does for everyone who embraces it. I had a new appreciation for nature and a theology that finally made sense to me. I felt empowered!

So why wasn't I getting the same kinds of magical feelings that everyone else always described? I never physically felt anything in circle. Forget seeing energy. I never heard the voices of the gods or saw visions. I'd worked successful spells—at least, I was pretty sure I had—but I didn't have the kinds of bodily experiences that other people, both online and in person, always seemed to talk about.

Maybe I just wasn't a real Witch. Or maybe I just wasn't a talented one.

I struggled with these feelings for years. I went to a lot of open circles, Pagan Pride Day rituals, and sabbats at Unitarian Universalist churches, and in every community I had the same kinds of experiences. Other attendees talked like they got so

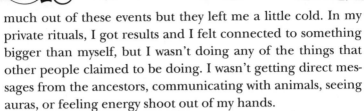

much out of these events but they left me a little cold. In my private rituals, I got results and I felt connected to something bigger than myself, but I wasn't doing any of the things that other people claimed to be doing. I wasn't getting direct messages from the ancestors, communicating with animals, seeing auras, or feeling energy shoot out of my hands.

I came to the conclusion that I just wasn't very magical. At first I felt bad about it, but then I decided to embrace it. Even *Buffy the Vampire Slayer* had Xander, the nonmagical member of the group. He didn't have superpowers, but he was still an important member of the evil-fighting team. I could just be Xander. That would be okay, right?

I made a lot of jokes about being a "brick wall" where magic was concerned. I started taking on ritual tasks that were difficult for other, more sensitive people. I could handle charged magical items with no effect, which meant I was great at dismantling and disposing of things. I could be around anyone without being overly impacted, which meant I was great at talking people down from highly charged emotional states after workings. I was immune to any kind of possession, which meant that in trance ritual I was great at spotting and taking care of others. I was always grounded. I seemed to be able to send energy (at least, I could work magic), but I wasn't receptive to it. At least now I had a place in my community!

Fine, but for a young Witch this was still infuriating. I mean, who doesn't want to have powers? I kept on with my studying and my practice. I joined my first coven and studied with my first teacher. I moved away. I found new communities and new mentors. Eventually, I was initiated into a traditional Wiccan coven. I kept reading, kept learning, kept practicing. Finally, so gradually that I barely noticed it, things began to change for me. I wasn't a brick wall anymore! Ritual had more meaning. My magic was more effective. I could feel things and had a better sense of what people meant when they talked about moving energy. What was weird was that there was no revelation, no

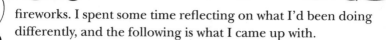

fireworks. I spent some time reflecting on what I'd been doing differently, and the following is what I came up with.

Allow Your Experiences to Be Different

One of the reasons I thought I was so inadequate was because I was looking to have experiences just like everyone else's. I was so focused on what other people said they were feeling that I was ignoring what I was experiencing. Everyone perceives energy a little differently, so when people talk about "energy," that could potentially mean a lot of different things. Some people experience energy as hot or cold. Others feel pressure, like something is touching their skin. You might feel lightheaded or suddenly very focused. Some people describe the feeling of something pushing against the back of their head. You might be one of the few people who actually sees energy, but overwhelmingly people don't. It took years, but I finally realized that movement is the key for me. I have a hard time generating power just standing still, which makes things like visualization hard for me. If I'm able to run, walk, or dance, my experience of ritual is totally different. I would never have found that out if I just did what other people were doing all the time.

Practice! Like, For Real.

I wasn't always totally honest with myself about how much effort I was putting into my Witchcraft practice. I mean, all the books say to meditate, but who really does it? Was I really sitting down every day to practice my magical skills? A lot of the time, the answer was no. Studying with a coven and being held accountable by other people helped me develop better habits. Now, that doesn't mean everyone needs to run out and find a coven, but it's always great to set practice and study goals and then find a way to achieve them. For me, mentors helped. For you, that might mean keeping a planner and actually scheduling time. Figure out what works for you and do it! Magic is amazing, but it's also work!

Keep a Journal

When I first began practicing Witchcraft, I got really excited about the idea of keeping a Book of Shadows and collecting spells and rituals. But years later, the stuff that's actually been helpful is the writing I did about myself and my own growth in the Craft. Not the stuff I just copied from somewhere! When I became more serious about documenting my feelings and my progress, I got to know myself better, and one of the central tenets of magic is self-knowledge. It seems obvious now, but at the time I was surprised that journaling could be so helpful in developing my magical sensibilities. It helped me track patterns, reflect on things that worked (and things that didn't), and notice stuff that I was just ignoring before. So if you don't already, keep a journal! If you're not much of a writer, try

scrapbooking, vlogging, or keeping a sketch diary. The format doesn't matter—just the results!

It's Not a Contest

Here's the thing I didn't want to believe as a newcomer: sometimes people lie about their experiences. A lot of us are attracted to magical practice because we've struggled in life and we finally feel like we've found a place where we can belong. When we want to fit in, it's tempting to exaggerate in order to impress our fellows. Sometimes in those moments when we're all standing around after a ritual and talking, it's easy to fall into the trap of one-upping each other in magical ability. I've heard people claim to be able to throw fire, to read minds, and to see the gods incarnate whenever they call. Far be it from me to tell anyone where the limits of magic lie, but use your good judgment here. Sometimes the reason we feel bad about our own magical abilities is because we're not very realistic and we're spending too much time comparing ourselves to others. My practice improved when I stopped turning my fellow magicians into my competition.

Magical practice is different for everyone. For years, I felt like I was getting it wrong and like maybe I didn't really belong, but all I really needed was time and better habits. Once I had a better sense of who I was and started paying better attention to myself, things started changing for me. I still can't see auras or hear godly voices, and I still sometimes leave rituals feeling like things fell flat for me, but I know now that it's not because I'm a brick wall where magic is concerned. I know what works for me, and I know that I'm actually capable of a lot more than I originally thought. The same is true for you!

Belly Dancing in Ritual

Estha K. V. McNevin

There has been a shift in the global reality. This New Age is blossoming into that first flush of consequences when growth and adaptation don't always make for good bedfellows. Letting go of the old ways is hard when in modern Pagan culture we have only just now managed to revive them. As our information and technological advances evolve, embracing a future for our Pagan communities means learning how to keep the religious techniques that really work, while evolving beyond defunct systems of doctrine or control. Our new rituals should bring us knowledge, life experiences, and joy by filling us with a sense of purpose and happiness in being alive.

Learning to Move with the Times

In my own community, adaptive and healthy New Age values have caused something of a pink revolution, in Hindi called a *gulabi kraanti.* The women in our coven, in particular, seem more committed than ever to self-adapting. We long for a rising up of integrity and accountability. Out of a deep need to hold a line of justice, we know that we dance our magick against a social backdrop of fanny-grabbers and gender-defined remits. This year we have enacted a dance class every Dark Moon, and we encourage all genders to practice body fitness and fluid movement during this time of humble New Age growth and evolutionary transition.

We have taken belly dance, one of the oldest types of ritual dance, out of the modern performance arena of sexual display; instead we use it as a gnostic or mystical tool of ritual. For us as Hellenic Pagans, it is an offering to our ancestors, planetary deities, and the gods of the zodiac. Especially for young girls coming of age, we matriarchal Pagans hope that our younger sisters and daughters will choose to belly dance for themselves with spiritual reverence, as if no one but the Goddess is watching. We encourage members of all genders, ages, abilities, shapes, and sizes to get their wiggle on. We have chosen to dance just to experience being alive and feel our bodies moving around to the rhythm of our environment. We engage dance in ritual as a fluid gesture that observes time and space in relativity to our own emotional spectrum and moods. We dance to feel the Force; we dance because it feels good.

Who cares how it looks to any critical mind? This type of praying with our bodies, through the language of gesture and movement, is very old and comforting. We have returned to our most basic human roots of cooperation in hopes that it will relieve this global sexual tension and bring greater levels of human rights and equality to our world. Perhaps simply by expressing our emotions and learning how to work together to celebrate life, we can come to better value and respect each other.

The Strength of Movement

Body shame was the breakfast, lunch, and dinner rhetoric of my youth. It shaped me in all the awful ways one might expect: it was guilt, binge eating, and abject shame on repeat until I discovered a more sacred path to life and began to exercise with yoga and belly dance. I didn't know women with my body size were considered beautiful until I was well into my thirties, and even then I struggled to believe it. I had been told so often that I was an unhealthy, ugly, and an unnatural abomination. A later exploration of my ancestral history helped me understand my body's own starch and sugar needs: my Scottish Highland family baked with oat, rye, and barley and sweetened everything with honey for three thousand years.

It took me a long time to get over the image of a lazy, fat, stupid girl that others had imposed upon me for so much of youth. Through that well-labeled lens of obesity, anything close to genuine self-esteem seemed impossible to cultivate from something as simple as learning and practicing a few dance moves. Believe me when I say that dance has served to shatter some of the worst of my fears. In fact, ritual dance has liberated me from a lot of social judgment and ridicule. In countless ceremonies, my spirit has been elevated to that mystical state; I have been moved by ancestors and gods alike. I have learned to use my feet for primordial magick, offering these footsteps to deities who really only speak in the language of dance to begin with. These old gods of the wild primordial earth are among my favorite to work with because they, like Lady Gaga, know that I was born this way for a reason.

There is nothing like that feeling of having danced for hours, sweating away every drop of your stress and fear, while the pull of the music lets you trek round and round the circle. Like a sweat lodge, ritual dance improves and tests our spiritual endurance. As a public display of devotion, it is an open physical investment of energy into the magick at hand. These primordial dance-based ceremonies at our temple are among the first to make me feel happy and alive. Rituals such as Bast Going Forth from Bubastis, on the fifth of December, are filled with joy and reverie because the goal is truly to invite the goddess of cats (the real rulers of the household) to feel joy through us. As we enjoy dancing and prancing along with her, we get a deeper sense of how to celebrate life together.

During Bastet's sacred ritual, we fill our dance card with rounds of play-pretend Nile River swimming, wheat planting, grain harvesting, and agricultural weaving dances. Some of these gestures are among the oldest in human culture. Every time I dance them, I feel that there is a deep sense of intuition and repetition in them that many of our ancestors surely also find comforting. When I am filling my imaginary basket with fruits and swishing my hip at the same time, it really makes me feel that pep in my step that comes from harvesting the garden for fresh vegetables. Dance often utilizes our physical and emotional memory to enliven our perspective on the world. And then there is the flush of all those lovely endorphins!

Cleansing the Body

We can get so weighed down by the details of our ancient and complex religion that sometimes we might worry more about amassing an esoteric library or tool collection than about developing our core body strength. Nevertheless, our health is an essential component of our magickal prowess. Nurturing our physical well-being with diet and exercise and fortifying our spirit by sweating out toxins is essential magick. Like many other Witches, I find that dancing helps me experience and create my own "scent cloud" or aromatic bubble. This

A LITTLE BIT OF MAGIC

Do let your heel and arch the corpus of the earth find. Open up your shoulders, elongate your spine, lift your toes nine balanced times.

is a protective and communicative pheromone cloud that is always around us. It is the physical part of our aura and is released by our body heat. Our scent is our strongest primordial marking tool, and it carries our magickal signature. It lingers on our objects and plays a strong role in how others instinctively respond to us.

Should we eat really fresh foods, this aromatic biosphere atop of our skin smells inviting and even alluring to others. But when we are unhealthy, our own sweat is full of fatty acids and compounds that are flushed from us in a great wave. Working out and steaming our bodies is an energetically healthful way of maintaining a positive and inviting aura because it promotes healthy bodily microflora and allows the natural muscle drive of the lymphatic system to flush all sorts of hormones and toxins.

Belly Dance as a Feel-Good Custom

When we work just three times a week to feel our moods and express ourselves using our bodies, even a little exercise can help us keep immune to a number of toxic emotions and negative circumstances in life. This is because when we elevate our heart rate, our brains produce norepinephrine, that shrewd "get up and go" substance that is triggered in fight-or-flight mode. Once all danger has passed, our brain will release serotonin, giving us those euphoric feel-good vibes. It's like a little reward for being a survivor. This mild mood elevator is a real powerhouse of self-esteem. You too can tap into the river of empowerment and survival like Beyoncé. In fact, tapping into your own body power with dance is one of the most ancient ways to celebrate life while also building up a heady dose of serotonin.

Along with improving our mood, dance helps us feel more physically grounded in our bodies, thus giving us a better sense of body control and balance. Being in tune with your abilities is the difference between knowing you can stick the landing on a leap versus just taking it wishful thinking. Given that dance can be low-impact and gentle on the joints, it really is accessible to anyone of any age. The longer we dance, the more it helps to lengthen and straighten the spine, adding to our overall body strength and greatly improving our hand-eye coordination.

Dancing with zills and swords work hand dexterity and finger strength, while hip movements are known to strengthen the legs and back. The three main regions—shoulders, hips, and thighs—are broken into up and down, left and right, and forward and backward hemispheres of the body. Each area is then worked in a wide variety of combinations to create a routine that expresses the mood and rhythm of the accompanying music. Each dance expresses a specific song or theme. Many ancient cultures still teach body language as dance, promoting more empathetic social and moral values that feature group unison along with individual self-discipline and personal sacrifice.

American Tribal Style Dance in the Twenty-First Century
Syncretic global fusion culture has become a hotbed of rhythm and art in our New Age. From Ibiza and Goa to Burning Man, the new age of peace, love, and understanding is alive and well within the global rave culture. This youth movement has given birth to modern improvisational styles like hula-hoop, hip-hop, tribal, neo-Polynesian and Afropop dances. Many of these are combined with tribal seasonal

or root dances, mudras, temple theater, Romani, burlesque, or Rajasthani Gypsy dances. Artists use modern Technicolor costumes that literally glow in the dark! American tribal styles of dance are pared with subculture music like goth, techno, and industrial genera because they are new cultural and sound experiences. This style of dance is known for intricate bodice and costume work along with glowing body paints, props, and tattooed or pierced dancers.

Many of these fusion styles celebrate colonial adaptation and use improvisational and live revivalist interpretations to traditional music and folk dances. This creates once-in-a-lifetime performances that are offered up in chirps, whistles, mudras, clicks, and skirt flips to indicate, redirect, or enact intentional magick. Group routines work off of each individual's talents and provide featurette rotations to give each dancer a chance to dazzle the audience. Organizations like the global Red Tent movement favor this style of dance because it highlights the genius we experience when we learn to dance together using improvisational cues. The high energy and adaptive movements make American tribal styles innovative and wildly entertaining. No two shows are ever exactly alike. From belly rolls to twerking, mastering the art of rhythm exchange and deep tempo keep these dances evolving with our global society.

The Magick of Mood and Movement

No one really knows how long humans have been belly dancing. There are few written records that date it to a single region of the world, and most of the sources that claim its origins are fraught with cultural or religious bias. Suffice it to say that the history of the dance is often included alongside those first secret mystery schools of women, where the recipes for beer, bread, and herbal remedies were shared alongside animal husbandry, textiles, and gardening. By 3000 BCE, the art of belly dance was widely practiced from India to the western tip of Portugal and stands as an original global exotic art. Even today, each style of belly dance features techniques and costumes that have a footprint in the Old World. Many have rules about the type or style of movements that are accepted, and others have mandates of when they may be performed and for whom. It is vital to take the time to research dance and truly commit the mind, body, and spirit to working together to learn the ins and outs of belly dance. Understanding each style is crucial to applying them effectively to ritual.

The difference between global cultural inclusion and privileged cultural appropriation is to be found in the details of a thing. You can't "fake it until you make it" with ritual dance; respecting the origins of a profound art such as physical worship begins with an open willingness to understand other cultural perspectives on life. Each new style of dance requires an ongoing and self-motivated type of adaptive cultural learning to truly master. When we approach it with humility and respect, dance is a magical linguistic curiosity, really, one that drives us to discover the world through the mesmerizing gnosis of shared movement. It has a universal appeal, and this is why it is a beloved type of performance art. Learning dance in this esoteric way truly puts poetry into the motions we master.

The following list breaks the basic movements of belly dance into elemental rulership and gives ritual examples of when and how to use the style to augment the energy of ceremony. Costumes and a certain flair for theater are prerequisite to including dance within ceremony. Things must be set and staged for success, or half-hearted attempts will cause the ritual's energy to fall flat and participants to feel defeated. To ensure success, practice for twice a week for one lunar cycle, even if it's just for an hour or two. Working your muscle memory two or three times a week is all it really takes to master any dance. Consistent self-discipline is an essential element of any success, even more so with dance. This is how belly dancing looks so incredibly controlled and fluid as a general rule. Muscle memory and control are in fact a long-term goal. We only get there through a kind of constant psychic vigilance—not by event-based pressure but by healthy weekly and daily habits.

Percussive Movements

Music: Staccato and scale
Element: Air
Planets: Mercury, Venus, Uranus
Zodiac: Gemini, Libra, Aquarius

Used to Evoke: Communications, siblings, marriage, partnerships, union, goals, friends, hopes

Themes: Shared group thoughts, instinct, self-improvement

Movements: Hip drops, hip rocks, outward hip tilts, hip lifts, hip twists, rib drops, shoulder rocks, outward rib tilts, shoulder lifts, shoulder and rib twists

Energy: Lift and drop to the beat to push, pull, and send magickal energy toward the past, present, and future; as above/so below on repeat

Ceremonial Styles: Drum-heavy shamanic work, high-energy rituals, and large group gatherings where seasonal themes are physically interpreted to affix a sense of purpose both magickal and mundane. Beltane and Yuletide can most especially employ these movements to express the heartbeat of the earth and the rhythm of life.

Fluid Movements

Music: Long lines of lyrical or modulated melody

Element: Water

Planets: Moon, Pluto, Neptune

Zodiac: Cancer, Scorpio, Pisces

Used to Evoke: Family, domesticity, security, passion, death and re-birth, soul, sacrifice, solitude, privacy

Themes: Group empathy and shared collective experiences of birth and death

Movements: Lots of abdominal muscle elongations; horizontal hip gestures suggestive of exploring or grounding; arm work featuring long vertical lines; hip circles weaving the magick of creation; hip, shoulder, and rib loops with repeating patterns of love and light; belly, thigh, and arm undulations to evoke empathy and compassion; improvisational and textured movements set a tone or mood that is felt by all present

Energy: Continuous slowed motion used to impart ethereal wonder and an element of mystery or fantasy

Ceremonial Styles: Rituals that require motion expressive of purpose or intent are empathic for audience and dancers. They are times of deep emotional connection, and a there is a sense of creation or birth that goes along with this style of physical expression. Rituals like Samhain and Ostara have an otherworldly feel about them that is ideal for lyrical dance. Complex hand movements and flowing costumes help elevate this style to near intoxication as participants become transfixed by the flow and tides of the dance.

Shimmy Movements

Music: Percussive cymbals, top beats, and scales

Element: Fire

Planets: Mars, Sun, Jupiter

Zodiac: Aries, Leo, Sagittarius

Used to Evoke: Appearance, image, identity, romance, creativity, children, travel, philosophy, education

Themes: The hot intensity of control and focus builds excited group states of cocreative manifestation.

Movements: Relaxed straight-legged, knee-driven, or hip-driven re-petitive vibratory motions; tensed straight-shoulder arm-driven or rib-driven syncopated and rapid motions; shimmies; shivers; vibrations; bouncing; hip, thigh, and bottom twerking

Energy: Growing to a crescendo, this energy is slowly built into rapid and repetitive undulations that excite the room. Playful and joy-ous, it must never be overemployed, as the ritual space will fall flat if the audience is overstimulated. Careful buildup and re-lease assures that the room feels a sense of energetic climax that is sexual and creative in nature, enticing even.

Ceremonial Styles: Oh, how the shimmies draw that survival energy right out of our chakras and into the room. These moves are de-signed to elevate the energy and raise the vibration as our kund-alini is awoken. This style of dance features strongly in shamanic ceremony and is used for Lammas, Bubastis, and Lunar New Year ceremonies at our temple.

Floor Work Movements

Music: Scale, melody, and lyric

Element: Earth

Planets: Venus, Earth, Saturn

Zodiac: Taurus, Virgo, Capricorn

Used to Evoke: Money, possessions, tools, routine, service, healthy habits, fame, achievement, mastery

Themes: Grounding and stabilizing; bringing a solid sense of what is real or bonded to the moment in union, contract, or Christen-ing/Wiccaning

Movements: Floor and body dancing; downward gestures; leg, arm, and hand tension followed by release and reversal of gestures; kicks, splits, bends, and drops; tea trays, swordplay, fans, veils, and wings

Energy: Earthy and grounding, these styles take the self-discipline of body control to the next level by adding an element of chaos, should the dancer lose focus. This feeling of direct consequences for failures of mind-body-spirit balance imparts a certain amount of tension to the dance.

Ceremonial Styles: Ideal for building and promoting holistic spiritual consciousness, these moves are often employed for rituals that seek to raise our vibrations or elevate a sense of possibility and opportunity. They are favored for events like Midsummer and Midwinter as well as on the equinoxes because they physically illustrate the razor-fine edge that exists between dualities. This 'twixt and 'tween magick has long been a core feature of Mercurial and transgender magick; many of the world's greatest dancers employ a modality of gender fluidity to master tea pouring and sword dancing, most especially.

Selected Resources

Constantine, Storm. *Sekhem Heka: A Natural Healing & Self Development System.* Stafford, UK: Immanion Press/Megalithica Books, 2008.

Lox, Curt L., Kathleen A. Martin Ginis, and Steven J. Petuzzello. *The Psychology of Exercise: Integrating Theory and Practice.* 4th ed. New York: Taylor & Francis Publishing, 2014.

Rose, Sharron. *The Path of the Priestess: A Guidebook for Awakening the Divine Feminine.* Rochester, VT: Inner Traditions, 2002.

Scully, Nicki, and Linda Star Wolf. *Shamanic Mysteries of Egypt: Awakening the Healing Power of the Heart.* Rochester, VT: Inner Traditions/Bear & Company, 2007.

Workplace Magic

Deborah Castellano

The workplace is full of challenges that you must face during your daily grind—the rumor mill, who gets chosen for the choicest projects, the draconian methods of getting promoted, nearly impossible work environments to endure to prevent yourself from losing a steady paycheck. Lucky for you, you can use Witchcraft! Take both practical and magical steps to help you look forward to the work day in the morning.

Solutions to Stop Workplace Gossip

First, start practically. Invite suspect(s) out to lunch. Don't bother trying to address the issue because in all likelihood it would instead be an exercise in blame-storming. It can be difficult to get to the root and even harder to know what anyone's intention was. During lunch, just be as charming as you can be, if you know what I mean. Think old-movie charming like Audrey Hepburn or Spencer Tracey. Project an energy of likableness. Be as fun and outgoing as you can be, and the suspects may then think more kindly toward you because of that energy or because you both like *The Real Housewives of New Jersey*. The whys matter less than the results here. When possible, offer to do the jobs that no one wants to do, whatever that is in your office. For me it was dealing with other departments, filing, and so on.

Then, try these magical approaches:

Stop Gossip Spice Mix

Literally break bread with your coworkers. Bake something, a quick bread, cupcakes, box mix—whatever. Just be sure you add Stop Gossip Spice Mix to it. You'll need these:

1 piece whole cinnamon
3 cloves

1 teaspoon allspice berries
1 teaspoon brown sugar

Get a coffee grinder and grind to a fine powder. Add 1 heaping tablespoon to your baking project. As you stir the batter clockwise, put your intention into it. The brown sugar is important because it will sweeten their dispositions toward you, the cinnamon is for fast action, the cloves are to stop gossip, and the allspice is for good fortune in business and money matters. As you are baking your project, focus on putting your intent into it—that these people will like you and be favorably inclined toward you in business matters.

Bring it to work the next day. Offer the project to everyone who is giving you a problem, coworkers and superiors alike. Leave what's left in the break room.

Sweeten the Workplace

Make a honey pot with the intention of sweetening your workplace in your favor. You'll need the following:

Small jar of honey
Small bowl
Brown paper bag
3 cloves
3 cardamom seeds
3 chamomile flowers (from a tea bag, if need be)
Small green taper candle
Carving tool

Take the jar of honey and empty about 1 tablespoon of honey into a small bowl. Put the bowl on your altar as an offering, and if you can, dispose of it by putting it by your workplace door (outside). If you can't do that, just put it out on a crossroads somewhere.

A LITTLE BIT
OF MAGIC

Incorporate color magic into your workplace wardrobe to add extra power to your intention. Red can be worn for leadership, green for transformation, blue for tranquility, and purple for smooth communication.

Get a small piece of brown paper bag that will fit in the jar and write the names of everyone causing you problems three times. While you are writing, do not let your pen leave the paper—neatness doesn't count here; continuity does.

Put on top of the paper 3 cloves (to stop gossip), 3 cardamom seeds (to attract good luck), and 3 chamomile flowers (to protect and keep money). Roll the paper toward you while setting your intention for job security, for the gossip to stop, and

for these people to feel "sweet" toward you (the purpose of the honey). Put it in the honey jar. Screw the lid back on the honey jar tightly. Put the honey jar in your sink or cauldron (someplace it will be safe, as we are about to get fire involved here).

Now take the small green taper candle and carve a symbol or words for what you want into it, and be sure to pray over it as well. Light it off your stove if it's gas; use a match in the kitchen if it's not. Let a little wax melt onto the lid of the jar and anchor the candle on top of the jar. Let the candle burn all the way out (I recommend getting a small taper for this).

Put the honey pot on your altar. Be sure to continue burning candles on top of the jar with symbols and prayers once a week to keep the mojo going.

For Steady Income

Try these everyday tips and spells for maintaining or seeking a steady income:

- Get a quarter coin from every working adult in your household. Put it in a shot glass. Put a mirror under the shot glass to magnify the effect. Cover it in honey. Set your intention over it. Clean it out and replace it with new honey periodically.
- Get two lodestones that are magnetized to each other. Feed them gold filings on a weekly basis by sprinkling filings on the stones.
- Get a High John the Conqueror root. Feed it weekly with High John Oil by sprinkling the oil on top of it.
- Glue a mirror onto your stove so that it reflects your burners, which will bring you prosperity.
- Keep a cedar tip in your wallet.
- Etch symbols and words that are meaningful to you into a green candle. Dress it with cinnamon oil and dab the oil in the direction that moves toward you. Light it off your stove if it's gas. If not, a match is fine. Burn a new candle weekly.

Enduring a Difficult Workplace Environment

In one of my old jobs, the moment the employees were put in a seminar and asked to talk about our workplace difficulties, everyone's response to me was always that I should look for another job, except for the instructors, who have seen enough hot messes to know better. It's not actually a helpful response to many of us in a difficult work environment. My old position was part of a dying field, but I made decent money and had good benefits. My husband was finishing school for a better career for himself, so it wasn't exactly the best time for me to rock the boat. It is such a 1986, privileged thing to say to a person about work or home life decisions when you don't have all the information that I immediately lose respect for the other person when it's said. "OMG, Betsy! Thank God you have distilled my incredibly nuanced problems at work and/or home down to such an easily managed proposition that I totally have not thought of! I would have never ever thought of leaving if you didn't point out to me that that's an option! You are such a godsend. Nay, savior."

Sometimes, all we can do is learn to endure. Many of us weren't taught that about the workplace, but it can help us get through the hard times. But that doesn't mean you have to just sit there and take it. Yes, you will sometimes need to appear as a supplicant to survive in the workplace. That said, it doesn't mean you shouldn't have a plan past *all your jokes are so funny and you are so attractive and smart*. It doesn't mean that you shouldn't have an end date for yourself in dealing with these shenanigans. You need to do more than just get through the day. You know what practical things you are supposed to be doing. Find out what your options really are to escape by arranging your finances, looking into secondary income streams, getting your physical appearance in order for interviews, talking to professionals as needed (therapists, lawyers, accountants, stylists)—doing what you need to do. Figure out what you need to be happy. Really happy, not Facebook or Instagram happy. Start making that happen. Do what you are supposed to be doing.

Get your magic in order. Trouble with someone wielding power over you and being a jerk about it? Hit up your recent ancestors. The ones who remember you as a tiny adorable baby. The ones who always cheered for you. The ones who always slipped you a twenty when you needed it. Tell them about your problems. Bring cake. Catch them up on the family gossip. Let them take care of it. If how they will take care of it worries you, ask them not to do X or Y. Or leave it to them if you trust them like that.

Stop living like a filthy hamster at work. It's not good for you. Wipe down all your surfaces with antibacterial wash. Keep your work area neat so that gross energetic dust bunnies aren't collecting into larger, grosser entities and making your life harder. If you

are like me in my last job and have people constantly dropping files and other debris on your desk like you are their personal garbage dump, take care of it as soon as possible and hand it back. If you have little actual personal space to call your own, start thinking small and what you can get away with that's vaguely office-appropriate New Age. Work over these items like it is your literal job at home, which is not a toxic cesspool, unlike work. Consider a salt lamp. It can actually do something for the air, it's only minorly weird, and it's a huge hunk of salt to banish negative crap from your space.

Resurrection Plant

There was no direct sunlight at my desk previously, so I bought myself a clear glass ramekin and a resurrection plant, which is obtainable online or at your local Witch shop. You'll need:

Resurrection plant
Ramekin
Rose quartz
Small mirror

The resurrection plant goes into the ramekin with the rose quartz with the round mirror under it to magnify all the positive vibes that me and the plant can muster up. And when your workplace inevitably tries to kill it, that's okay! Your plant is coming back to life! What now, crummy workplace?

Not having sunlight is a great reason to give for why there's a resurrection plant on your desk. Plus, anyone with an Instagram or a kid with an Instagram will just assume you are suddenly very fashionable. Whatever. Stop soaking up all the negative vibes into yourself like that is part of your actual job description and focus on what is actually in your job description and work to keep the rest out. Just because you are handed a bag of rocks doesn't mean you have to carry it.

Water Magic

Magical Self-Care
for Hard Times

Mickie Mueller

Into each life some rain must fall, and the life of a Witch is no exception. We do our best to keep our energy positive—we go to work, pay our bills, and try to treat others with kindness—but sometimes the universe has other plans and things unfold in ways that we didn't expect. Hard times can happen to anyone. It's nothing personal; it's just life. As magic users, we have a few extra tools for managing the challenges of life as they unfold, but because of the spiritual work that we do, we can also feel more vulnerable when things go awry.

Magical self-care can empower you when facing big challenges like a financial crisis, divorce, or medical issues. Sometimes hard times hit us out of the blue. How we handle them can affect the outcome. It's a knee-jerk response to either overreact or shut down in confusion or panic, but by mindfully using self-care techniques such as meditation, crystal healing, aromatherapy, support from loved ones, and shielding from negativity, we can embrace our power and navigate the sometimes-troubled waters of life.

Have I always been an expert at doing what's best when the chips are down? Absolutely not. But I've been through my share of crazy stuff, so I have learned a thing or two over the years and I'm happy to share. I've had deaths in the family. I went through a rather icky divorce and an even more icky arrest of my then ex-husband, family drama, a broken arm, and a couple cases of precancer and invasive cancer of my cervix, which lead to two surgeries right before I decided to write this article. I know a little bit about the benefits of self-care during hard times, and as it happens, I've learned how bad things can get if you choose to ignore self-care. Been there, done that. Trust me, the first rule is this: if you don't take care of yourself, you can't take care of anyone else!

None of these methods should be used by themselves; if you need a lawyer, doctor, financial adviser, or professional therapist, use common sense and get the everyday help you need. In addition to mundane assistance, you can add magical techniques to lift yourself up and help you overcome your challenges more successfully. When a mess hits the fan, it's time to Witch up.

Meditation Anyone Can Do

Okay, I know, some people are big meditators—others not so much. It can be more difficult to quiet your mind when you have worries, but it's the time that you need it the most. Meditation can really help your mind rise above the fight-or-flight response, which is just part of our biology. Fight-or-flight is hardwired in. If you start to feel panicked, don't blame yourself—it's okay. This automatic reaction

and quick release of adrenaline helped our ancestors survive when a saber-tooth tiger was stalking them. Unfortunately, this response doesn't really help us in a courtroom, at a doctor's office, or when getting chewed out by our boss. We can't run from these situations, and punching someone would just cause more problems. Instead we internalize that energy, and what can result is panic or anxiety. Meditation can bring us back to where we need to be physically and mentally so that we can deal with a situation in an appropriate way.

If you don't really meditate much, think you're not good at it, or you're experienced but having trouble because of stress, try a meditation app or guided meditation videos online. A friend of mine suggested an app for my phone called Insight Timer that was free. You can choose guided meditations, music, and more, and you can choose the duration as well. Even a five-minute meditation can be helpful. I found one to literally talk me through a panic attack when it's happening, and it worked quickly. I bookmarked it so that it's always at my fingertips should I need it. I even found singing bowl recordings on the app that aligned with different chakras, so when I was preparing for and recovering from my surgeries, the sacral and root chakra singing bowls were my saving grace. There are other apps too, such as Calm or Headspace. Find the one that you like and use it. You don't have to be an expert to use a guided meditation, and when you're under pressure, it's nice to have that voice to talk you through.

Nourish Yourself

I don't know about you, but when I'm stressed out, I want to eat cake. I know you read that as a slice of cake . . . but I meant *a* cake. They don't call it comfort food for nothing. It can really help your body and your magical energy if you make good choices for meals and snacks, but that can be an extra challenge during times of stress. My suggestion is if you want cake, eat cake, but pick up one cupcake from the bakery and turn eating it into a ritual and savor it so that you get all the comfort you need, and then make some healthy choices after that. Of course, this goes for ice cream, chocolate, mac and cheese, or whatever your food vice is—have it and enjoy it with no guilt and then be done with it.

The other side of that coin is the people who can't eat when they're stressed out. When life is getting you down, focus on making sure that you're eating regular meals; even if they're small meals, you need to nourish your body. It can be easy to skip meals when you have a big crisis to manage. Stock up on the things your body needs instead of starving or eating your emotions. Making mindful choices can really help your magical energy. Low-fat proteins and fresh produce can feed your energy instead of deplete it like junk food. As magic users, we need to revere our bodies as sacred, and that means feeding it fuel that can get us through every day and keep our energy running smoothly.

A Little Bit of Magic

CHAMOMILE LAVENDER TEA IS A GOOD STRESS REDUCER, AND THESE HERBS CAN MAGICALLY HELP CURB EMOTIONAL EATING CHALLENGES.

Another thing you can do to nourish yourself is to drink lots of water. Water helps flush out not only physical toxins but also emotional toxins from your energy system. The best way I've found to make sure I'm hydrating is to carry around a refillable water bottle. Then I know how much water I'm drinking and it's more convenient. You can draw magical symbols for health, blessings, or protection on the bottom of your water bottle and empower every sip with magic. If your bottle has a little loop or clip on top like many of them do, you can hang a little magical charm on it. I made a charm out of a cage pendant to hang on my water bottle and filled it with small tumbled stone chips. Stones to boost your healthy habits and healing include amethyst, agate, rose quartz, apatite, and turquoise.

Cry, Scream, Vent

The pain caused by difficult times can sit inside of you and eat away at your well-being. There are situations when you need to keep your feelings inside, put on your game face, and just power through, but it can become a problem when you try to do that all the time. A strong psychic shield to keep negative influences out of your energy field can also keep any negativity you're generating trapped if you're not clearing it regularly. I know this because I did it for years during and after my previous marriage. I thought I needed to stay strong for my kids, and I just kept the act going all the time. If your mantra is *it's okay, everything's fine* when the room around you is on fire, you might want to rethink that. You can smudge your house all day long, but if you're keeping negative emotions inside, you can't clear your life and be empowered.

If you have a trusted friend that you can vent to, that can be helpful. Let them know ahead of time: "Man, I really need to vent.

I've got a lot inside that I'm dealing with, and I need to get that out." Make sure they understand that you may not be looking for solutions; you just need help releasing some negative emotions and talking it out. When you're done, sip some tea together, light some cleansing incense, and clear it all away. If you don't have someone you feel like you can share with, consider a professional counselor or therapist. I'm really over the stigma associated with mental health—as a society, we need to be over it. We're not embarrassed to go to the doctor with a sinus infection or broken bone because getting help when you need it is not a weakness but a strength, and that goes for mental health too. I went to a therapist earlier this year to help me through some tough things that resurfaced from my past that I didn't deal with at the time. Talking it through really made a difference. I wish I had done it years ago.

What else can you do to release difficult emotions? Cry in the shower; it can be very cathartic. If you're having trouble releasing a good cry, try watching a movie that always makes you cry just to break the seal, and then you can let loose. Tears are very cleansing.

Find a private place to scream your head off. Yell about how angry you are at your situation, how it's not fair, how you're tired of not getting a break, and how you don't deserve this. Let it all out.

After you're done releasing emotions, take a magical bath. Try sea salt, Epsom salt, a chamomile tea bag, and a couple sprigs of rosemary. Call in your spirit guides and deities of your choice and charge the water to clear any lingering negativity in your aura. After releasing trapped emotions and cleansing, you'll feel relieved and better able to face the hard stuff you're dealing with.

No matter how you choose to clear out your difficult emotions, make sure you do it. Ignoring what's inside and hiding it away can lead to constant microaggressions leaking out, lack of sleep, and drained energy.

Find Your Happy Place

When we have big challenges in our lives, we often go into survival mode, and it feels like we can only do the minimum for ourselves just to get by. We tell ourselves, "Once I get through this bad thing that's happening, maybe I can start to be happy again." I know that it feels that way, but finding little bits of happiness every day can lift you out of survival mode and make hard times more manageable. Take a ten-minute break and walk in the park and instead of dwelling on the problems, and ask your higher power to show you the beauty in the world. Watch for little treasures—a feather on the ground, a sparkling stone in the path, a bird singing in the trees.

Music is another way to lift your spirits. I like to play music when I'm cooking and sing along. I find this puts magic and love into the meal and really lifts my mood. In your downtime watch a comedy, something that will make you laugh out loud. Laughing is very healthy: it releases endorphins, reduces stress hormone levels, and even boosts your immune system. I often pick a comedy series and watch one episode every day while I eat my breakfast, and it sets the tone for the day. Here's a magical idea: choose a citrine crystal and hold it every time you watch a comedy and charge the crystal with your laughter! Carry it with you when you need to keep your heart lighter or laugh in the face of adversity. You'll have your laughter crystal full of joy and humor.

If I'm in a really dark place, instead of complaining about it on social media, I like to post something positive on my accounts, the kind of thing that I would tell someone else in my place to help them out. It's a magical practice because first I'm sending something positive into the world, and then it makes other people happy too. They react and comment, and that interaction boosts the good energy I'm putting out there. Often people tell me they needed to hear the message too, so then suddenly, by trying to make myself feel better, I've made someone else feel better too. That's magic!

Oils, incense, and aromatic herbs are mighty magical ingredients, and there are so many ways that you can use them. One of my favorites is to create a simple spritz using the oils of my choice, adding a few drops to a travel-size spray bottle full of water. For joy and blessings, try frankincense, bergamot, rosemary, lavender, sweet orange, or angelica. I add a bit of vodka to extend the life of magical sprays. Be sure to shake it before using. Spray yourself, the room, your car—wherever you need a bit of magic. Another great way to use magical oils is by anointing candles with oils specific to your needs and charging them with your intentions. If you need to de-stress your environment at work or at home, try an oil diffuser. It's a really easy way to fill the air with happiness while making magic.

Enchant the Heck Out of Everything

Here's a story that I hope inspires you to use magic to manage a challenge by enchanting things you might not think of enchanting and working within the energies of the moment, instead of trying to fight every step of the way. I bet you can apply these concepts to other situations.

I was going in for my hysterectomy, and I was instructed that I wasn't going to be allowed to wear any jewelry, lotions, oils, or hair products—none of that stuff. No pocket full of stones for this Witch, no mojo bag in my bra, no Fast Luck Oil anywhere on me. Here's the thing: my surgery was scheduled during Mercury retrograde,

the astronomical event that happens several times a year when the planet Mercury appears to go backward in the sky. It's a period of time that's notorious for communication mix-ups, mechanical problems, and monkey wrenches in the works. Also, it was one of those robotic surgeries. Yes, I made plans to be stabbed by a robot during Mercury retrograde. Did this Witch panic? Oh hell no, I just started thinking about ways to make this work for me.

None of my usual witchy tricks could be used, but I had been given a bottle of antiseptic body wash that I was supposed to use all over in the shower right before I left to go to the hospital. I grabbed a permanent marker and drew magical symbols all over the outside of the bottle. I charged it with Reiki, set it on my altar, and charged it with protection and healing energy. When I used the wash that morning, I asked Mercury, as his planet traveled in reverse, to help me safely release what I didn't need in my body anymore.

My surgery was also the same day as the lunar eclipse, July 27, 2018, which was the longest total lunar eclipse in the twenty-first century. I swear I didn't plan that. The night before my surgery I charged a compact mirror under the Full Moon with the intention for healing energy, and I packed it in my hospital bag. After the surgery was over and I was in my room that afternoon, the eclipse was happening on the other side of the world. I opened my compact mirror to channel the energy of the event, releasing that which didn't serve me, transforming toward cronehood, and healing. I'm writing this one month later, on the Full Moon, and I'm happy to say the surgery was a success and I'm healing very well.

That's how I managed to come up with ways to work my magic even in the middle of a crisis just by thinking outside the box. You can do it too. Use common sense to take care of yourself and boost that care with magic when you do. You can get through anything that life throws your way if you take the time to value yourself and enchant your life. You're so worth it!

The Magic in Numbers

Charlie Rainbow Wolf

Have you ever heard of numerology—the study of the significance of numbers in your life? Even if you haven't, chances are you've noticed how certain numbers keep repeating themselves, or maybe even how they influence you. Numerology is based on your date of birth (the time and place aren't important in this instance), your name at birth, and also the name you use now. It's a fascinating study, because math is a universal language, and numbers reveal so much about any given situation if you just take the time to learn about them.

Number by Number

The Number 1

This is the beginning of things. When you learn to count, you start with 1. In fact, nearly everything starts with 1; the first steps of a project, the first month of the year, the first day of the month or week. It's the number of purpose, of starting out toward an end goal. It's not fussy about what stands in its way; it will simply find a way around, over, or through any perceived obstacles. The magic of this number is found in its simplicity, straightforwardness, and sincerity.

The Number 2

I think this number looks like someone knelt in prayer, head bowed. That sums up the magical energy that it brings to the circumstances that surround it. Its vibration is humble and graceful but by no means weak. It's supportive and creative, charismatic and intelligent—although when backed into a corner, 2 can be needy and show its temper! On the whole, though, 2 is a good mediator, and its strength is found in its kindness.

The Number 3

In math, 1 + 2 = 3, and it's the same in numerology. The number 3 is assertive and dynamic like 1 but also kind and moody like 2. It flits from one situation to the next, weighing them all up and getting too occupied with the minutiae to see the bigger picture. This is the enigmatic energy of 3, both its asset and its liability. On the one hand, things are never dull, but on the other, there may be a lack of focus. Wherever 3 stands out, you're going to need to cultivate some discipline!

The Number 4

I bet the bed you sleep in has 4 legs and the vehicle you ride in has 4 wheels. This epitomizes the stability of 4. It brings order and stability wherever it's found. It shows you where you're going to be working hard, perhaps too hard; don't let 4 tempt you into becoming a workaholic! Its magic is in its stability, not in its seriousness. You might have to work with some of the lighter numbers like 3 or 5 to help 4 loosen up and evolve.

The Number 5

This is another lighthearted and unpredictable number. The magic 5 brings is that it thinks outside the box, takes the risk, and breaks the rules—and usually has a lot of fun doing it. It usually carries above average luck too, which makes it welcome, albeit a bit frustrating with its lack of discipline at times. The 5 indicates instability and change, so don't take things too much to heart as they ebb and flow. If possible, add 4 or 8 to help discipline 5's devil-may-care energy.

The Number 6

The 6 is a very nurturing number and is happiest when it's looking after someone or something. When you see 6, you know that nurturing abounds. The magic of 6 is sensitive, sometimes over-sensitive, and gets its feelings hurt easily. It keeps on giving until there's nothing left to give, and if it's not appreciated, it will turn sullen and downcast. It has big ideas and high ideals, but they're often too hard to live up to.

The Number 7

Throughout history 7 has been seen as kind of a mystic. In Roman mythology Hercules had 7 labors, and there are 7 chakras that run up the spine. It is definitely unique, and its magic is one that highlights where you or your situation may be quirky or abstruse. It doesn't seek to be the center of attention, but more often than not it finds itself there simply because of its charisma and intrigue!

The Number 8

Tilt an 8 on its side and you get the lemniscate, the symbol for infinity. The 8 brings infinite potential, but it's a disciplinarian and will make you work for your rewards. Its magic lies in its karma—

and karma doesn't have to be a bad thing. This number is just the law of cause and effect. As the old saying goes, the harder you work, the luckier you'll become. Take responsibility for everything you are and everything you've done, and 8 will work with you toward a successful outcome.

The Number 9
Just as 1 is a beginning, 9 is an ending, because after 9 we get into double-digit numbers. When 9s are repeated in different areas of your life, you know that change is afoot, and it's time to let go of what's no longer viable. The magic of 9 is that it's dignified and chaste. This is also a hindrance at times, because 9's energy does have a tendency to get snooty if not balanced with other numbers.

The Master Number 11
In numerology, the standard is that every compound number is added together and reduced until a single digit is reached, except for the case of the master numbers. These are 11, 22, and sometimes 33. The number 11 draws attention to itself because it's a unique blend of both 1 and 2, where there's both the dynamic energy of the warrior and explorer and the charismatic charm of the hopeless romantic. You'll have to make sure you don't overthink things when 11 is present, because if you do, it will create self-doubt and steal away your confidence and chances for success.

The Master Number 22
This master number is a marriage of the signatures from 2 and 4. It is dreamy and creative, but it also has the foundations of practicality to put down roots, and get things done. Its magic is that it brings the potential for fabulous change. Open your eyes when you see 22, because it will be easy to be blind to your talents and abilities to get things done. You'll have to stay focused if you don't want to leave a myriad of unfinished projects in your wake. Lighten up a little and cultivate some faith in your capabilities.

The Master Number 33
There's some doubt about whether 33 is actually a master number or not; I'm going with it depends on the circumstances! Tradi-

tionally, it's not included, but in more recent times it's been making an appearance. (Some even go so far as to include all double numbers, such as 44, 55, etc. My own opinion is maybe in the future numerology will evolve in that manner, but I'm sticking with 11, 22, and sometimes 33 for now.) The 33 is enigmatic and difficult to incorporate; there's a definite lack of focus here. It's able to completely leave one reality behind and exist in a totally separate realm, which is another reason it's so challenging: we live in the physical world. I encourage you to only count 33 if there are other master numbers with it; if it stands alone, reduce it down to 6 and interpret it that way.

Putting It All Together

When you start to understand the magical impact of numbers, you can start to apply it to your daily life. One way to do this is to look at the significance of the calendar numbers and use numerology to calculate the most favorable dates for rituals, spellcasting, and more. You might even want to take into consideration the numerical value of the hours in the day, as well as the date, so that you get the most benefit from their vibrational influence.

Do bear in mind, though, that numerology is more than just the date on the calendar or the hours on the clock. You have your own numerological cycles, and they're going to be different from anyone else, because you're unique. Consider planetary weather and astrological aspects too. Numerology is just one facet in the myriad of forces that affect you and everyone else every moment.

Day by Day

Every calendar month brings you a new opportunity to learn something new or do something different. You can hedge your bets as to what dates are good for succeeding by applying some basic numerology. Most people make New Year's resolutions because that's the first day of something new. The first of the month and the first of the week are often popular. If the first of the month and the first of the week coincide, then you get a double dose of that dynamic energy of 1! Let's look at what the days of the month have to offer, according to their numerological resonance.

The First

Get going! You have a vision and you're keen to get ahead. The 1 brings a sense of "let's do this," but you may be lacking when it comes to patience or cooporation with others. Avoid arguments, because they could permeate through the rest of your endeavors if you're not careful. A bit of honey in your tea or spinach in your salad will go a long way to keep this day on track!

The Second

This is the day for taking time to think things through. People might be more open to new ideas and more receptive to your plans and projects. If things went awry yesterday, this is a good day to try to fix them. Don't hesitate to reach out to people on the second. Avoid people and foods that are hot and spicy. To keep the day balanced, wear orange, eat orange-colored food, and drink orange-colored beverages.

The Third

Conversations and communications of all kinds are favored today, as is anything to do with creativity and self-expression. Remember that words are only a small part of the way that you convey messages to others, and put as much effort into your body language as you do into what you say. There's a lighthearted energy with the third, but it may lack substance. Counteract that by surrounding yourself with yellow and wearing or carrying tourmaline.

The Fourth

This is the day for stability and focus, as well as a fantastic day to start something you want to last—providing your personal numerology and astrology are in agreement! There's dedication bordering on stubbornness today; don't forget to consider others before you barge ahead to execute your plans. Diffuse some of that energy by wearing soft greens and avoiding people and foods that are overbearing.

The Fifth

This is often a lucky day, one where you feel alive, capable, and ready to take on the world. Overindulging in the physical senses may distract you from your responsibilities, though. See if you can invite a more stable energy by wearing shades of green or pink (which also happen to be heart chakra colors).

The Sixth

Today is favored for gathering with loved ones. The emphasis is on making people feel good about themselves, and that includes you too! Work hard to put out any fires that arise, sensitivity is strong, and folks could take things too personally. Wear onyx or obsidian to help you to ground your own energies while at the same time assisting you in deflecting any negativity from others.

The Seventh

This is another lucky day, bringing with it flashes of clarity where before there's been uncertainty or obstacles. You're probably best keeping yourself to yourself. If you do have to associate with others, schedule some downtime, and have a place where you can retreat

and recharge your energy. Balance the vibration of 7 out by ensuring you get enough sleep and proper nutrition today. It will be easy to try to cut corners; don't.

The Eighth

The 8 is a number of movement and motivation, and today is no exception. There's a bossy and overbearing energy today; make sure you're not buying into it and being bossy yourself. Cultivate patience and understanding while at the same time focusing on getting things done. This balancing act might be a bit easier if you can make it meatless or carry some smoky quartz with you when dealing with others.

The Ninth

Daydream much? This is the perfect day for spending time on your own and indulging in some self-expression. Keep at least one foot on the ground, though, because you may be more accident prone than usual. Balance this energy by wearing things in fours: jewelry that has four stones or clothing that has four colors. Grounding stones such as tourmaline and obsidian will help too.

The Tenth

The 10 takes the energy and action of 1, and then the 0 placeholder amplifies it. You're likely to be on fire with enthusiasm, but it will be easy to spread yourself too thin today because so many opportunities look intriguing. Overcome this by looking for 2 to bring some balance and duality: wear jewelry or colors in pairs, and choose simple rather than complex recipes to eat.

The Eleventh

The first of the master numbers! There's an abstract and utopian vibe in the air today. You may be a bit more on edge than usual, or perhaps you notice everyone else being a bit uptight or excitable. You can't do much about what they do, but you are in control of how you respond to it. Lots of fresh food and soothing colors will help you to deflect the nervous energy.

The Twelfth

This is a blend of 1, 2, and 3! Make time to examine your feelings. Folks are likely to be moody, and if you're one of them, get it out of your system with some kind of artistic activity. Connecting with your feelings and expressing them in a constructive way is vital today. Wearing yellow or carrying a piece of citrine works in your favor to make the most of the opportunities today's energy brings.

The Thirteenth

The key numbers here are 1, 3, and 4. There's nothing unlucky about the thirteenth, not even on Friday—unless you happen to be a fourteenth Knights Templar! Just be careful to examine everyone's motives, including your own, and neither take advantage of anyone nor let yourself be used. Wear and eat lots of green to keep the energies harmonious.

The Fourteenth

The 1, 4, and 5 make up the mix of energies today. There's a restless energy running through things that could result in broken promises and lots of frustrations. The dominant 5 requires real effort to stay focused. Do your best to stay connected to your obligations and to others, and don't get too attached to things you can't control. Wearing gold jewelry or orange clothing is beneficial.

The Fifteenth

The numerical vibe of this day is focused on 6 with 1 and 5 playing a supporting role. Nurturing is important, for both you and those in your life. A little compassion will go a long way today. Don't isolate others; just make sure that your own needs are met first. You may tire easily. Lots of fresh fruits and bright colors will help, as will wearing red clothing or jewelry.

The Sixteenth

The 7 is the dominant vibration today, with 1 and 6 throwing their nuances into things just to make them interesting. It's a day for facing your procrastination and accomplishing something. Once you start, you'll find the task flows easily and absorbs you. Don't get

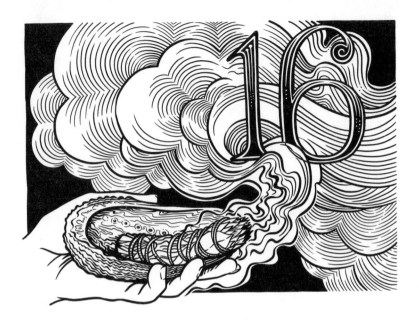

so consumed by it that you become oblivious to all else, though. Burn a little sage in an abalone shell to keep the aura clean and harmonious.

The Seventeenth

Today's main player is 8, which brings that businesslike and sometimes cold efficiency. The 1 adds determination, while the 7 throws aloofness and detachment into things. Watch for bossiness today, coming from yourself or from others. It's a good day to get things done, organize, and prioritize, but there may be a clash of opinions. Keep things smooth by wearing green or carrying a piece of rose quartz.

The Eighteenth

The number 9, with all its knowledge and poise, is the leading energy for today, supported by 1 and 8. Take the initiative and reach out to someone, but make sure that you are offering an olive branch and not starting a fire. It's easy to be a bit pompous or over-critical with this combination, so keep your words sweet and try not to judge others. Eating or carrying garlic is favorable.

The Nineteenth

This is an enigmatic day, for 1 is the dominant number, being two out of the three numerical influences (the other being 9). Independence rules, but try not to be too overindulgent. Let others have their way, within reason—it frees you to do your own thing. Stay away from rich or fatty foods today, and watch your alcohol consumption. Remain in control without being controlling.

The Twentieth

Today is the energy of 2, magnified and augmented. Conflict arises out of moodiness and comes quickly today, so you'll need to stay grounded, centered, and shielded in order to stay on top of things. Emotions are supercharged, so start the day off with meditation or prayer, and keep tapping into that higher energy as the hours pass.

The Twenty-First

The main theme of today is 3, social and gregarious, with 1 giving it direction and 2 maybe making you a bit sensitive. It's a good day to relax, which is awesome news after the heightened energies of the last few days. Socialize with whom you want, but don't be pressured into anything. The color red helps you motivate yourself, as there's a touch of laziness here.

The Twenty-Second

We're back to a double dose of 2, with 4's hard work and determination for today. Intuition and hunches will guide you through today if you let them. Give others space to do likewise. Step out of your comfort zone, but only within reason. If you need a boost, try using mint in some way—a tea, a sweet, or even an essential oil in a diffuser.

The Twenty-Third

The key frequency for today is 5, with sensitive 2 and convivial 3 adding some interesting overtones. Sensual pleasures are heightened and extravagance comes effortlessly today. Bring in some discipline by staying focused on the long-term goals. Wear black or carry a black stone to remind you to stay grounded and determined.

The Twenty-Fourth

Today's main vibe is nurturing and caring 6, with 2 reaching for the stars while 4 keeps things practical and grounded. This is a good day to listen to others, but not for taking sides. People will take advantage of your good nature if you let them, so don't let them. A quartz crystal is a good talisman to carry; imagine it as your armor against unwanted attention.

The Twenty-Fifth

This is a lucky day for the most part. Lucky 7 is the star, with sensitive 2 and frivolous 5 livening things up a bit. Throw yourself into learning something new. Today isn't particularly favorable when it comes to matters of the heart. Don't take emotional upsets too personally; burning a pink candle will help you to find your center again.

The Twenty-Sixth

There's an odd energy here, because the star of the show, 8, is a bit overwhelmed by the more sedate energies of 2 and 6. You'll start to see what needs tidying up before you can move on, but impatience is likely. People may get bossy or bombastic about their needs and desires. Keep out of the drama by holding your tongue and wearing purple.

The Twenty-Seventh

The number 9 always has a ring of truth around it, and today is no exception. You could hear some unpleasant news today that, even though you know it's right, you just don't want to accept. Work with the supporting energies of 2 and 7 to ensure that you see the bigger picture and that you're gentle with yourself while doing it. Work with the heart chakra colors of pink and green to keep things uncomplicated.

The Twenty-Eighth

We're back to all kinds of 1 here. Newness and eagerness permeate the day, but try not to be too keen. The 8 makes it easy to be thorough and businesslike, while the 2 gives you a sensitivity. Put that to work or the overall energy gets irritating and restless. Start the day with a mantra of kindness and goodwill, and repeat it throughout the day when things start to vex you.

The Twenty-Ninth

This is a compound energy with 11 being the main focus, but 1, 2, and 9 all want their say—particularly 1! Don't rush into anything today because it might not be what it appears. Today brings you opportunities to lead by example and be a positive influence on others. Ensure your words match your actions and wear red to draw the right kind of attention to yourself.

The Thirtieth

The order of the day is 3, magnified, highlighted, and perhaps a bit out of control. Self-expression rules; you may be rushing to finish month-end tasks, but you still need an outlet for your creativity. Try journaling out your thoughts at the end of the day; it's purgative and sets you up nicely for the following newness.

The Thirty-First

This is a blend of 4's dedication, 3's nervous energy, and 1's enthusiasm. It's important that you relax and don't let yourself succumb to being overworked. The world is unlikely to stop just because you did, but that's not an excuse for laziness, either. Earthy colors, natural foods, and being outside in nature will set you up for tomorrow's newness.

Conclusion

Of course, not everyone is going to have exactly the same experience on the same day. In numerology, this is one area of study but not the only one. Your personal cycle, pinnacle cycle, life path number, and even the calculation of the universal date will all have an impact on how the day unfolds. It's a fascinating study, one you might want to dip your toe into by observing how the energy signature of the days of the month influence you and others in your life.

Mirror, Mirror:
Some Common Superstitions

James Kambos

A broken mirror. Shaking a rug outside after dark. An owl hooting nearby in the night. Or a passerby who gives an unusually long, lingering stare.

For most people, these seemingly common occurrences are no cause for alarm. But some people, who view these events as *omens*, or portents of a coming disaster, take these happenings quite seriously. The belief that a certain occurrence has a supernatural cause and is a sign of coming misfortune, even death, is known as a *superstition*. Superstitions have existed since before recorded history.

In some instances, superstitions were used to explain an unusual event in nature. For example, if a bird flew into a house, the residents would naturally be surprised. But if someone living in the house suddenly became ill afterward, the people in the home may then believe that the bird was a warning of the coming sickness. For many, the idea that a bird flying into a home forewarned the illness seems silly. Some also explain it as simply a coincidence.

However, many people believe that we are surrounded by signs and messages from the supernatural realm. For them, superstitions are taken very seriously. Two of these people were my grandmother and my mother. If they saw, heard, or experienced anything they thought to be a bad omen, they would begin a folk magic ritual to avert disaster. Or, they'd pray, run for the holy water, and grab the nearest black veil! They knew, they just *knew*, tragedy was about to strike.

Even though many of us don't believe in superstitions, their meanings and origins are very interesting. So, follow along with me as I take a look at some superstitions that my family firmly believed in. I'll try to unravel some of their origins and, where possible, explain why they frighten us.

Mirror, Mirror on the Wall

Reflective objects and surfaces have been surrounded with mystery and superstition even before mirrors were created. Many of these beliefs concerned the human soul. It was thought that a reflective surface, such as a body of water, glass, a polished stone, or a mirror, had the ability to capture the human soul. If anything happened to the reflective surface—such as the mirror being broken—as someone gazed into it, the soul, it was thought, would be trapped. Then, upon death the person would be soulless and unable to enter the next realm, since their physical body had been separated from their soul.

Almost everyone has heard about the superstition that breaking a mirror will bring seven years of bad luck. How did this get started? It probably began in ancient Rome. The Romans believed the number seven represented a complete cycle. They thought that after a serious illness, the body took seven years to heal. They also believed, for example, that after the land had been ravaged by fire or pests, it took the earth seven years to achieve growth and harmony again. In numerology, number seven also symbolizes completion. For example, there are seven days in a week, and so on. So, a seven-year cycle of bad luck after breaking a mirror begins to make sense.

Now, how can you reverse the curse of seven years' bad luck after breaking a mirror? Some magical traditions believe in removing the reflective quality of the broken pieces remaining from the mirror. To do this, smash the remaining pieces into useless fragments. Once it can no longer reflect, the mirror is considered powerless.

Here is one more recommendation: Gather the broken pieces. Wrap them in black fabric or newsprint and bury them. The fabric or newsprint will absorb any bad vibrations, and the earth will cleanse the broken mirror of any negativity. If possible, do this during a Full Moon.

It doesn't matter if you believe that a mirror can capture our souls or it can cause seven years' bad luck when broken. It's amazing how reflective surfaces of all types have captured our imaginations for thousands of years.

Broom and Carpet Superstitions

Brooms and carpets have long been associated with magic and superstition. A broom (besom) has naturally been linked with Witchcraft, folk magic, and superstition over the years. Carpets have also been a part of magic—think flying carpets—as well as superstition for centuries.

I learned about broom and carpet superstitions at an early age. I was taught as a child to never sweep around a single woman with a broom. To do so, I was told, would mean she'd never marry. Growing up in Appalachia meant I also knew about the superstition of placing a broom across your front door. This was done to keep out black magic.

To *jump over the broomstick* is an old wedding or hand-fasting superstition. At the conclusion of a wedding or common-law ceremony, the couple would jump over a broom together. This superstition was meant to bring fertility and good luck to the couple.

Due to their place in the home, carpets and rugs were sometimes surrounded with bad superstitions. Since they were meant to hold dirt and dust, they were also thought to attract and trap hostile energies. It's no wonder come spring, they were taken outside and beaten clean with a tool made for this purpose. The carpets not only received a spring-cleaning, but they were also cleaned of any negative vibrations.

But, one evening as I helped with the household chores, I learned you never sweep your front steps or shake a rug outside after dark. When my mother saw me sweeping our front steps and shaking the kitchen rugs outside after dark, she scolded me. She informed me that according to an old belief, I was shaking away our good luck. She said such cleaning should only be done during daylight hours. Later research, however, turned up another possible reason to avoid sweeping and cleaning rugs outside after dark. In Doreen Valiente's book *An ABC of Witchcraft Past and Present,* she explains that this superstition may have begun during the Irish Witch trial of Dame Alice Kyteler. Dame Alice, it seems, would sweep the streets after sunset. It's said as she did, she'd whisper a charm while sweeping toward her son's front door. It's possible that after this the superstition began, so to prevent being accused of Witchcraft, people started to avoid sweeping or cleaning rugs outside after dark. We may never know the reason for sure, but I do know my family would never do it!

And here's one last broom superstition my family believed in: when you move, never take your old broom with you—leave it or throw it away. Always start your life in a new home with a new broom. In other words, make a fresh start.

A LITTLE BIT OF MAGIC

To see yourself sweeping with a broom in a dream means you'll clear away a lingering problem in your life. If the broom appears to be new, the problem will fade quickly.

Bird Superstitions

If birds, as I mentioned earlier, do something out of the ordinary, many people become alarmed. The reason many individuals believe in bird superstitions is because birds are thought of as supernatural messengers. This probably comes from birds being associated with the sky, flight, and air. For this reason, if a bird flies through an open door or down a chimney, some folks fear the worst. If a bird flies repeatedly into the same closed window, this too is considered a bad omen.

Some people are in fact so afraid of bird superstitions they won't even use a bird motif in home decorating. I once had a bird come down my chimney and land in my wood stove. Needless to say, my family was in an uproar, but honestly, nothing bad happened.

The owl is the one bird most deeply associated with superstition. The belief that an owl heard hooting in the night is a death omen is widespread. Owls, being nocturnal, are thought to be messengers from the Otherworld, hence the death omen belief. I once heard an owl hooting after dark in a Florida marshland and thought it to be quite beautiful.

It's a shame that our beautiful friends, the birds, can inspire such fear. Please remember, if a bird startles you with some kind of unusual behavior, think about this—they're probably frightened too.

The Evil Eye Superstition

The belief in the superstition of the evil eye is one of the most ancient and widespread beliefs known to the human race. People who believe in the evil eye believe that certain individuals have the ability to cast a spell, curse, cause illness, or send bad luck by giving someone a jealous stare or an evil glance. Anyone who may be the victim of the evil eye is said to have been "overlooked." It's also believed that most people who have the ability to cast the evil eye are unaware that they possess this unfortunate power.

For people from around the region of the Mediterranean, such as my family, the evil eye was serious business and a part of daily life. If you took ill suddenly, if you had a run of bad luck, or if your livestock took sick, the evil eye was suspected.

I was taught from an early age what to do to avoid becoming a victim of the evil eye. Basically, it boiled down to being modest and humble. I was told that people who bragged about their wealth were setting themselves up to be cursed by *to máti*, "the eye." Or if someone took too much pride in their looks, they may get hexed by the evil eye. I was never allowed to be too happy or to laugh too loudly. If I did, my mother would say, "Shh! You're laughing too loud. That's not good!"

Many of these beliefs can be traced back to ancient Greece. According to myth, the gods and goddesses became jealous if a mere mortal was too happy, too strong, too talented, or too beautiful. In a fit of jealousy, the deities might punish the mortal or turn them into an animal.

But we had ways to avert the dreaded evil eye. Charms and crosses made of that lucky gem turquoise were worn. Bright blue beads were carried at all times. Eye beads (I'm wearing one as I write this) were worn on chains. The idea is that the eye would "stare back" the evil. And front doors and shutters were painted bright turquoise blue to repel the evil eye.

Some families had secret spells to break an evil eye curse, but they were rarely shared.

$$\bullet\ \bullet\ \bullet\ ☽\ \bullet\ \bullet\ \bullet$$

As long as there is a human race, there will be superstitions. Some may be old wives' tales, and some may contain a kernel of truth. But they all serve to help us understand our uncertain world.

Resource

Valiente, Doreen. *An ABC of Witchcraft Past and Present.* Custer, WA: Phoenix Publishing, 1973.

Magick for Personal Justice and Judgment

Diana Rajchel

Eventually someone will do you wrong; that's life. That wrong goes beyond forgetting to say thank you or excuse me. At some point someone breaks your heart, breaks your car windows, or lets you know what they really think of you. Sometimes, in heartbreaking situations, you end up wondering what the right thing is, or if the best thing is also the wrong thing. That's life—even when you have all the things you need provided, something comes up that challenges the soul.

Often enough you can involve the law, confront the cheater, or ask for a refund. Even so, there are no guarantees that the mundane route can give you a fair outcome, and sometimes it doesn't. Magick is our recourse when achieving equity through the usual channels has failed.

Please note that I have thus far avoided use of the word *satisfaction*. Fair outcomes may not give you satisfaction. You could resort to hexing and cursing, and sometimes that may be exactly the right kind of justice, because it does fill a void within you. But if you practice a tradition of Witchcraft that believes in karmic repercussions, you need a different route.

If you want to ensure a fair outcome, opt for justice magick. In this approach all people involved with the situation are submitted to examination and energy/karma is then redistributed. If you do not entirely know what the right action or outcome is, you employ judgment magick—and then observe either instructions on right action or a message to engage in a justice working.

Before digging into justice work, please take stock of your own cultural beliefs about justice. We all have preconceived notions of "fair" and "unfair" that cosmic forces may not understand. This cultural difference can appear across different occult traditions, especially in those where righting a wrong done to oneself is perceived as a personal moral responsibility. What one Witch of one culture might label immoral might be considered exactly the right thing to do by a Witch in a neighboring culture. For example, if someone violates the law of hospitality by harming someone hosting them, some Witches might believe releasing a curse is a necessary act of long-term home and self-protection. A different Witch might simply cut the energy between the home and the bad visitors. There is no single universal code of morality and classification in magick because magickal practices do not share one single cultural context.

A general look at the spectrum might appear like this:

cursing   crossing   hexing   justice   judgment   healing

←——————————————————————————————————————→
                                                              *
DEATH AND   jinxing   *blessing*
VIOLENCE CURSING   *

You may already know what category your ethical quandary falls in. If you do not, the following questions can help you find clarity:

- Have I done everything I can to resolve this issue without magick?
- Will I feel the same way about this when calm?
- What have I lost? How deep is that loss?
- What have others lost?
- What can I and others lose if I take further action?
- Do I have all the information about what was done, why, and how?
- Do I understand the motivations of the person/people that hurt me? Do I need to understand them?

A Simple Ritual of Judgment

Judgment rituals usually feel simple and intuitive. Often when completed, practitioners feel a sense of relief and clarity. That clarity can sometimes be followed by pain: understanding a situation and its meaning can cut deep. Before you do this work, make sure first

that you really want to end confusion and have a plan to care for yourself after the work. You will need to address a deity or angel of judgment or wisdom. Possible deities include Zeus, Hanuman, Athena, and Anubis. Angels may include Phanuel, Azbogah, Ramiel, and Remiel.

You will need:
Image of the deity or deities you are petitioning
Heatproof container (A small cauldron is best.)
Salt
Bay leaves
Glass of water
Pen
Paper
Lighter or matches
Stick of resin incense such as myrrh, frankincense, or copal

This work requires deep focus. Turn off your phone, lock your doors, and give yourself a safe, comfortable space before you begin. Set up an altar with the image of the deity or angel of judgment behind the heatproof container. To the left have salt, to the right, bay leaves. Set your glass of water next to the bay leaves. Crack a window before you begin or perform this ritual outside if you can do so with a modicum of privacy.

Meditate for a few minutes, chanting the name of your justice deity or angel. When you feel a sense of "differentness" for the outside world, write your petition. Describe your situation, why you need clarity, and then make your request for judgment. Ask for a specific omen that indicates an answer to you. For example, you may ask to see a raven on top of your car if you are to move on to justice magick, or a dove or eagle in a different circumstance if the Divine wants you to let it be.

Place your petition in the cauldron and sprinkle the salt and bay leaves on top. Light the letter. Make sure the petition burns out completely. Pay attention to the smoke—white smoke indicates an acceptance of the petition, black smoke a rejection. If you receive a rejection on a judgment petition, this usually indicates that the outcome is not a matter for your involvement. If this is over a matter that affects you directly, this will happen only if you have false information about the situation.

At the last ember pour out the water and douse the flame. Meditate until the vessel has cooled.

When you can pick up the vessel without burning your hands, thank the deity, and light the incense as an offering. Clean up immediately after, burying the fire ash or scattering it at a crossroads. If you receive an omen while disposing of the ash, you may want to look it up in a dream dictionary.

Justice

Justice working requires a deeper commitment than that of judgment. In judgment, you hand off the energy to a higher power. In justice, you bring that higher power to your own plane. This demands more work, more thought—and gives more chances to reconsider.

Before beginning a justice working, meditate daily for at least one week. Use the time to explore what inner and outer forces drive you, identify what triggers this situation sets off in you, and consider every being affected by your actions, including pets. Entities aligned with justice don't grant clarity so much as they demand it.

Once you complete your week of meditation, the ritual takes three days to prepare and perform. The first day is for cleansing and clarity, the second for presenting your case, and the third to release yourself completely from the situation and invite restorative energy. Each act should take a minimum of one hour.

Day 1: Cleansing and Clarity
Bathtub or shower
Muslin bag with sea salt, alum crystal, and hops flower
Ritual knife
Clarity Oil (A bit of lemongrass in olive oil works.)
Seven-day white jar candle
Large bowl of water

Prepare a bath, tying the muslin bag underneath the faucet. If you do not have a bathtub, rub the bag over your body in the shower, moving from the top of your head downward. Imagine all the negativity you've harbored about the situation washing off you in the water. Pull the plug on the tub or turn off the shower and step onto a waiting towel. Take the knife and cut any invisible cords you imagine on your body—pantomime around the top of your head, your shoulders, your throat, your navel, and your heart and along the lines of your legs. Allow yourself to air dry.

Next anoint yourself with oil on the top of your head, between your eyebrows, over your heart, and over your belly. Rub a small amount of oil on the candlewick, light it, and carry the candle to a safe place to meditate. Place the candle where you can gaze at it comfortably. Relax, chanting,

Guide me to truth.

Allow the situation to play across your mind, imagining the flame eating any beliefs or feelings that stand between you and genuine insight.

Take at least 20 minutes, more if you have trouble maintaining focus. When you feel an energy shift, place the candle inside the bowl of water and let it burn. If at any time the glass burns black, you may need to repeat the cleansing bath, and you may wish to enhance your magickal protections.

Day 2: Presenting Your Case

The seven-day white candle, still burning in its bowl
Blue or orange glass jar candle in a bowl of water
Judgment and Justice Oil (Crushed bay leaves and a few cloves in olive oil works.)
Clarity Oil
Frankincense stick incense
Incense holder

Create sacred space in a comfortable place to meditate. Set the new candle in the bowl next to the still-burning white candle. Anoint the wick of the new candle with the Judgment and Justice Oil. Anoint your forehead with Clarity Oil. Light the frankincense in the incense holder and speak out loud to the justice deity or spirits. Tell them about the situation and explain why you believe justice is necessary. If you have done anything to gain satisfaction or revenge rather than justice, this is the time to confess.

Pay attention to any feelings of "differentness" after this. Meditate as the incense burns, and note any received images, thoughts, or sensations. When the incense finishes burning, thank the justice spirits and close the ritual, letting them know they will see you the next day.

Day 3: Cutting Yourself Off from the Situation

Scissors
Twine or thread
1 yellow glass jar candle
Clearing Oil (Use olive oil with lemon rinds, Epsom salt, and alum
    crystal mixed in.)
1 blue glass jar candle
2 bowls of water, 1 for each candle
A few juniper berries

If the situation is personal, cut a length of twine large enough to go around your wrist, allowing for about two extra inches. If it is for a larger concern, cut enough that the twine encircles your waist. Set this aside and anoint the wick of the yellow candle with the Clearing Oil.

Hold the twine between your hands and imagine your emotions coalescing into a single thread of color. Push that color into the twine. Make sounds, breathe in different patterns that allow the energy to release, move, stretch, and dance—keep directing that into the twine until you feel spent. Once you do, tie the cord around your wrist or your waist. Pick up the scissors and say,

Before the witness of justice, I cut myself free of this situation.

Cut the cord. Next, wrap the cord around the outside of the yellow glass candle, light it, and set it in the bowl. You may wish to burn another stick of incense and meditate, or you might choose to go for a walk outside to recalibrate your energy.

After an hour allowing the candle to burn, return to your sacred space. Prepare the blue candle and sprinkle the herbs on top very lightly, taking care not to drown the wick. Light the candle and say,

I receive restoration for what has been lost.

Meditate on the candle for about 5 minutes, then place it in a bowl of water.

Justice can be swift and decisive—but when it is slow, it is because something needs discovery. Let the candles burn. In the days after, turn your attention to the next thing in your life that needs attention.

$$\cdots \;) \; \cdots$$

Judgment and justice call for complex work not just on the outer world, but on the soul of the person that enacts this magick. The results are sometimes hard to accept, especially when you can't replace what you lost. Whatever brings you to need judgment or justice, take care of yourself. What is right or wrong constantly changes, but the need for healing remains eternal.

Coming Full Circle:
The Element of Spirit

Monica Crosson

When I look back at my life, I am flooded by a strange mix of emotions—a sweetness tinged with an empty longing for what could have been . . .

"If only." A wispy voice hangs in the distant corners of my mind. "If only."

As I write this I am sitting on a log at the edge of the forest, watching the river as it moves gently westward toward the Salish Sea. My three grown children are standing in the distance throwing rocks into its silty folds. Their voices roll across the riverbed and I am reminded of tiny hands and struggling feet as I, not so long ago, guided them to nature's classroom.

"Can we listen to the river's song, Mama?"

"Of course, dear one."

I blink back tears triggered by happy memories. The element of water has a way of tugging at my soul. I know that I have done well by them (though sometimes I question myself). I raised my children to respect humanity and nature, but most of all to love themselves for who they are—so they can better love others.

We eat a meal together on the bank of the river, as we have done since the kids were small. And though beef has been exchanged for veggie burgers for three of us, they're cooked on the same barbecue my husband made from a stump twenty years before. I know these moments won't last forever, and as we sit in the same dilapidated lawn chairs around a firepit whose stones hold so many family memories, I savor the banter and teasing and laughter that rise and linger like the smoke from the embers of our dying fire.

"I'm going to take the cooler back to the house," Steve says.

I nod and Josh splashes water on the last of the fire before he finds his siblings, who have rushed off. I am left alone with only the rushing of the river and the sound of a woodpecker tapping out a message in a nearby tree. The sound reminds me that the earth has a rhythm if you are silent enough to listen.

This thought takes me back to the garden—my solace and therapy. Elijah more than any has carried on our family's agricultural traditions. His major in school is environmental conservation, and he works summers as a farmhand at an organic farm. He's giving me tips now.

"Can you hear her earth beat?"

Tiny heads press against the soil. "Yes, Mama! The Goddess is alive."

My most treasured memories involve gardening with my children. The practice has helped keep our family grounded and taught us about sustainability and the importance of giving back to nature, as well as to one another.

My three grown children are standing beside me now. "Hey Mom," Chloe says. "We're gonna drive into town and see a movie. Wanna go?"

"I've got to get this done." I point to my notebook. "Did you ask Dad?"

"Yeah, Dad's going too."

"Have fun," I say.

They leave and their voices filter through the breeze until I am left in silence with only the soft brush of air against my skin.

"There's something in the wind," my grandfather's words sing softly.

"Yes, you were right, Grandpa," I answer the memory quietly.

This element more than any other has helped transform me, move me, inspire me to do things I never thought I was capable of. You reading this is an example of the magick of air in my life.

I look to my feet to find small toads have lumbered onto the beach—they seem to come from nowhere.

I laugh. "You guys! I'm warning you: I am clumsy, and I will step on someone."

As I move the small toads to a safe position under an elder tree and far from my footfall, I am drawn to the dimming light and the shades of orange and yellow that burnish the water. I walk down the riverbank to find a better view of the setting sun.

Watching the sun set into the western hills, I am reminded of the times in my life when I called upon fire to kindle strength when my courage had dwindled and I felt I had no light of my own to give. Memories of struggle upon struggle infiltrate my mind, and I feel the anxiety as it rises and sticks in my chest. I blink. Take a deep cleansing breath and release. "If only."

But the words quickly dissipate, and from deep within my soul there is a vibration that fills me with the assurance that every moment is a blessing—every season a lesson and through it all there is magick.

What Is the Fifth Element?

One description that I hear over and over concerning the fifth element, known as spirit, Akasha, or ether, is that it is nothing, yet it is everything—and this is true. It is invisible, yet it is the very essence of our soul-being; it is neither masculine or feminine, yet it encompasses all gender orientations. It is both projective and receptive. It is a state of unbeing, yet it is what binds all elements into one cohesive system. Simply, the element of spirit is the breath that gives life to magickal working.

When we call upon our deities, we are calling to spirit. It encompasses our souls, and when we are clear of mind and focused on our intentions, we can utilize this energy for positive results in our spellwork.

To connect with spirit, one must go within. It dwells in us as living beings, both when we are aware of it and when we are not; it provides spiritual balance and symbolizes transformation and transcendence.

Spirit is unlike the other four elements in that, since it is part of everything, to pin down specific correspondences is almost impossible. Its direction is none yet all. Its season encompasses the entire Wheel of the Year. Its energy is both projective and receptive, and its colors are black, white, and purple.

Akasha

Akasha, the name sometimes used for the fifth element, became known through a collection of anecdotal accounts and shared knowledge introduced to Westerners by members of the Theosophical Society. Theosophy was founded by Helena Blavatsky and became popular in the late nineteenth century. It is a system of philosophies connected to the origin of life, nature's intricate web and mysteries of the universe. The word *Akasha* is a Sanskrit word meaning "space" or "atmosphere" and pertaining to a nonphysical energy form that is present in all things. The Theosophists were greatly influenced by the idea that one could tap into a collective universal consciousness known as the Akashic Records. This collective consciousness is said to contain the energetic vibrations of every thought, emotion, and intent that has ever been manifested since the first division of oneness or Source. One analogy that has been used to help understand this concept is that of an internal library wherein we can tap into transcendental knowledge, human experience, and universal lore.

Akashic Thinking through Mindfulness

There have been many throughout history who said they were able to gain access to Akasha and extract information. There are some who claim that the advisors of the great pharaohs of Egypt were some of these people and that the Sanskrit language itself was developed by tapping into Akasha. There are even those in modern times, including spiritualists like Edgar Cayce and Dion Fortune, who lay claim to this feat. It has also been thought that the Book of Life mentioned in the Old Testament may be referring to the Akashic Records. Tapping into a universal consciousness might seem intangible and mysterious, but acquiring Akashic thinking through mindfulness exercises just might help get you there.

It can be particularly difficult to keep in our awareness in this busy, noisy modern world we live in. That's why meditation, prayer, and ritual are treasured practices among spiritual seekers of all kinds. When we become quiet and still or when we go to our sacred place—be it a favorite room, a space in your garden, or somewhere in the natural world—we can more easily get back in touch with Akasha.

One way to tap into Akashic thinking is through mindfulness techniques. Mindfulness is a form of meditation that is done by maintaining your awareness on one thing, typically your breathing. Being aware of our intake of breath and the slow release can help clear the mind and quell restless thinking. But just like any other form of meditation, it takes practice.

One easy way to practice mindfulness is by lying somewhere comfortable and taking a small pillow and placing it on your chest. Close your eyes and focus on your breath. Do you feel the pillow as it rises and falls with each breath? Focus on the weight of the pillow as it rises up and down and your mind begins to slow. Of course, removing all distracting thoughts from your individual mind is extremely difficult, but with practice and a willing spirit, you can access the perceived emptiness that will guide you to the Akashic mind.

Ether

The Greeks recognized a divine presence and worshipped many individual deities, so they knew that there was more to the universe than meets the eye. The word *ether* was applied to what the Greek philosophers saw as a kind of air that provides life to the divine. It was Aristotle who wrote in his 350 BCE book, *On the Heavens*, that there were five elements that compose this planet. He described the four classical elements of earth, air, fire, and water as perishable, while the first element, located in the celestial regions and heavenly bodies, was described as being neither hot nor cold, wet nor dry, and was the matter of which all other things were made up. The ancient Greek poet Hesiod in his work *Theogony* described ether as an allegory for light. Aether (Light) and his brother, Hermera (Day), were birthed by Erbus (Darkness) and Nyx (Night)—thus, darkness gives birth to light.

The Alchemist's Quest
The medieval alchemists who sought to define the substance (ether) that made up the heavens came up with the idea of a quint-

essential element, known as *quintessence*. Because this element was thought to have a pure and heavenly quality, medicinal alchemy strived to make quintessence tangible by distilling alcohol seven times. It was believed to cure all manner of illness and impurity, and the term quintessence has since become synonymous with elixir and the philosopher's stone.

Spirit's Sacred Breath of Knowledge

I know we have all done it (and if you haven't, you should). Take a beautiful apple from its tree, known as the silver bough or the tree of Avalon, and slice it crossways. What you end up with is a lovely representation of one of the symbols that we as Pagans hold dear, one that (for me) represents spirit's breath of sacred knowledge and the mysteries of the earth: the pentagram, laid out in a perfect five-pointed pattern of seed.

This upright five-pointed star wrapped in a circle, worn by Witches and used in spellwork and ritual, has a long history. The five-pointed star's symbology goes back thousands of years: in ancient Mesopotamia the star represented the five astrological directions associated with Jupiter, Mercury, Mars, Saturn, and Venus, which was revered as the Queen of Heaven. In ancient China the pentagram represented the five elements of water, earth, wood, metal, and fire. The Sumerians used a pentagram glyph to represent their word for *corner* or *nook*. In ancient Judaism, the star represented the five books of the Torah, and Christians used the five-pointed star to represent the five wounds Jesus had suffered while on the cross.

In sacred geometry, mathematical constants can express themselves in the form of patterns and cycles in nature; the pentagram is a prime example of this. The golden ratio,

A Little Bit of Magic

WHEN WE ARE CLEAR OF MIND AND FOCUSED ON OUR INTENTIONS, WE CAN UTILIZE THIS ENERGY FOR POSITIVE RESULTS IN OUR SPELLWORK.

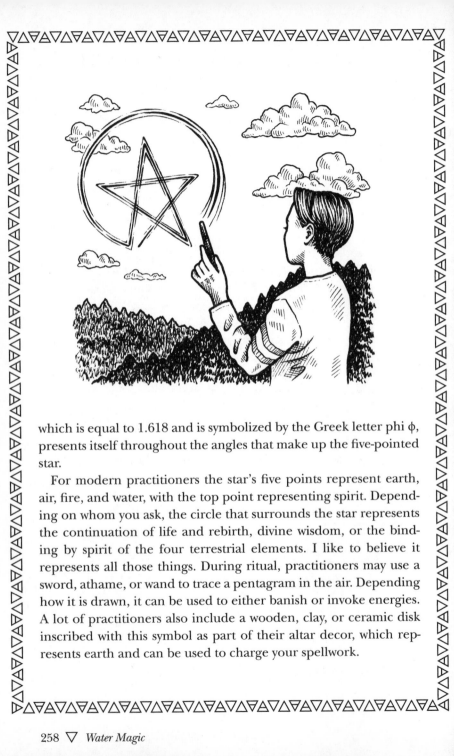

which is equal to 1.618 and is symbolized by the Greek letter phi φ, presents itself throughout the angles that make up the five-pointed star.

For modern practitioners the star's five points represent earth, air, fire, and water, with the top point representing spirit. Depending on whom you ask, the circle that surrounds the star represents the continuation of life and rebirth, divine wisdom, or the binding by spirit of the four terrestrial elements. I like to believe it represents all those things. During ritual, practitioners may use a sword, athame, or wand to trace a pentagram in the air. Depending how it is drawn, it can be used to either banish or invoke energies. A lot of practitioners also include a wooden, clay, or ceramic disk inscribed with this symbol as part of their altar decor, which represents earth and can be used to charge your spellwork.

Candle Magick for Divine Inspiration

This is a great little spell to connect with the Divine Spirit for inspiration.

You will need:

Sharp tool for inscription
White or purple votive candle
Sage oil
Appropriate candleholder
Pentacle-inscribed disk

Write an inscription representing spirit (to you) on your candle. Anoint your candle with the sage oil for universal wisdom. Place the candle in its holder and place the holder on the disc. As you light the candle, in your own way ask spirit to guide you along your spiritual path. As you watch the flames, imagine them igniting that spark of inspiration within you and feel the heat build up within your soul.

When you feel ready, thank spirit in your own way and let the candle burn out in a safe place.

• • • ☽ • • •

In one way or another we are seeking spirit our entire lives. But, as I have found, if you look inward, spirit is there. It is there when you call upon deity to enliven your magick, and it is there when we go within—it is that divine spark that guides us through life's transitions as we walk along the spiral path. It is that primal source of energy that binds the elements together, and it is there if only we seek it.

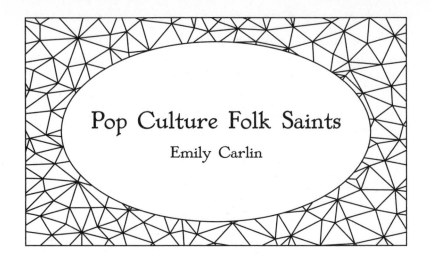

Pop Culture Folk Saints

Emily Carlin

We live in a world where celebrities and public personalities are often larger than life. Some popular figures can be so venerated that they become something positively magical—a pop culture folk saint. A mindful and respectful practitioner can work magickally with the energies of these amazing people just as they would a traditional folk saint.

What Is a Folk Saint?

For those who are not familiar with Catholicism, *folk saints* (also called *popular saints*) are dead people or spiritually powerful figures who, while not officially canonized by the Church, are celebrated as saints by popular consensus. While common in most Catholic traditions, they are particularly popular in Latin America, where they are exemplified by figures such as El Niño Fidencio, a deceased Mexican healer believed to grant miraculous healing to devotees; Juan Soldado, a deceased convict who is considered the patron of undocumented immigrants; and Santa Muerte, a spiritual entity that embodies the concept of death. They perform the same function as official saints, such as granting favors to petitioners and acting as intermediaries between devotees and God. Uniquely, folk saints tend to fill the voids in what is considered acceptable behavior by the official Catholic Church and serve those otherwise neglected or marginalized.

As with traditional folk saints, pop culture folk saints come into being when a beloved figure is raised to near-mythic status in the popular consciousness. When people become famous, it is common for them to develop a secondary public persona that is separate from who they are in everyday life, that exists in the minds of the public, and that is anchored energetically on the astral plane. That secondary public persona can, potentially, gain a life of its own and become a *thoughtform*—a separate magickal entity capable of being worked with by a practitioner.

For most celebrities these public personas are weak things meant only to protect the privacy and emotional core of the celebrity, but for a select few that endure over time and are fed by both the actions of the celebrity and the devotion of fans, they can evolve into something powerful. Think of megastars and public figures like David Bowie, Freddie Mercury, Mr. Rogers, Neil deGrasse Tyson, and Ruth Bader Ginsburg. These are all people who are popular in their own right, but they also stand for something much greater than themselves in the public mind. While a practitioner could, potentially, work with the public persona of any celebrity, success is much more likely with the potent persona of a cultural icon.

Much like their Catholic counterparts, pop culture folk saints rise up to fill the spaces not easily covered by traditional deities and metaphysical powers. The grand majority of Pagan deities and magickal powers are ancient—think gods of the sea or harvest, demons of precious gems, or mill faeries. As such, they can seem a bit removed from the everyday concerns of the contemporary practitioner, such as dealing with traffic, broken smartphones, or getting the kids off to school on time.

Pop culture folk saints are very much of the here and now and thus are much more closely connected and arguably more sympathetic to the needs of today. Certainly, a modern Kitchen Witch can work with Hestia or Brigid, but calling on Julia Child to help keep a soufflé from falling just seems intuitive—no mental leaps or reframing of ideas necessary. Similarly, a student can work with Hathor or Tianquiztli while studying for an astronomy exam, or they could work with the likes of Edwin Hubble or Carl Sagan. The one is not necessarily better than the other but may be more apropos. It is more logically direct to connect Thomas Edison, one of the primary developers of the light bulb, to electrically powered devices than Zeus, Greek god of lightning. While no one would say that modern folk saints are more powerful than ancient deities, it can be less of a stretch to connect them to modern priorities.

When working with a pop culture folk saint, it is important to maintain the separation between the public persona being called upon and the private individual on which the persona is based. Pop culture figures are or were living, breathing human beings. They are unique individuals with their own thoughts and feelings, and practitioners with no direct connection to those individuals have no right to energetically draw on or interfere with their energies. On the other hand, one can comfortably argue that their public personas are public property because they are made for the public and are often maintained by the energy of the public eye (as

well as the work of the celebrity and countless agents, PR consultants, etc.). When doing any work involving actual people or their personas, especially those still living, it is extremely important to ask permission and respect boundaries. Asking permission before working with any metaphysical entity is both wise and polite. A willing participant in a working will always give forth more effective and harmonious energy than one whose will has been neglected or coerced.

Explicitly working with the public persona, rather than attempting to work with the private individual, it is important not only to respect the folk saint but also to help the practitioner pinpoint the specific energies they wish to work with. Large public personas are well known and a practitioner can be confident that they know the energies they'll encounter when working with it. Private individuals are deeply complex and often unpredictable; one can never be certain what energies they'll get when drawing upon them. Before beginning any magickal working, clearly state that you wish to work with the elevated persona represented by the celebrity or explicitly say that you wish to work with them "as a folk saint" in order to maintain the boundary between the public persona and the private individual.

Working with Pop Culture Folk Saints

In practice Catholic petitioners work with their folks saints very similarly to how magickal practitioners work with spirits, loa, fae, or other respected magickal entities. Just as a magickal practitioners ask for the aid of metaphysical entities, folk saints are often called upon to give advice through signs and augury and to directly affect the mundane world in miraculous or magickal ways. Most Catholics petition folk saints for aid by reciting prayers, lighting candles, and making various offerings in exchange for intercession by the folk saint on their behalf. These same methods and variations thereupon can be used when working with pop culture folks saints.

Say a Prayer

The simplest traditional way to work with any saint or folk saint is to recite a prayer. In Catholic tradition there are specific prayers that are offered to each saint or folk saint. These are usually about a paragraph long and will (1) name the saint, (2) describe why they are considered holy and their dominion, and (3) briefly outline how the saint will aid the petitioner. Many of these prayers will also add a coda describing the specific ways the petitioner will thank the saint when their prayers are answered. While a prayer to a pop culture folk saint can be done in any style, it is fairly easy to create a pop culture petition in the traditional style. For example, if a practitioner wanted to petition David Bowie as the patron of creativity and self-expression, one could say this:

> *Oh Great Saint David, man who fell to earth and arose to stardust, you who defied convention to sing your truth to the world, bless me now with your gifts of creativity, freedom, and self-expression; help me find my true self and share it with the world.*

If old-world prayer isn't to your taste, it is also appropriate to style a prayer in the manner of the pop culture folk saint's favored speech patterns or vernacular, with the addition of quotations and catchphrases as is fitting. For example, to petition Nelson Mandela as the patron of convictions, one could recite this:

> *Nelson Mandela, stalwart heart that stands up for truth and leads by example, you who learned that courage was not the absence of fear but the triumph over it, that the brave man is not he who does not feel afraid but he who conquers that fear, bless me with the courage to stand up for my convictions and to fight for what I know is right; help me remember that it always seems impossible until it's done.*

A quick internet search should yield many quotations and interviews that can help inspire an appropriate prayer. However, there's no need to stress over perfect wording or imagery. Simple prayers that come from the heart and energetically connect to the pop culture figure will be effective.

Light a Candle

The most common way to petition a folk saint is to light a candle and say a prayer in their honor. While virtually any candle can be used in this way, most petitioners use the seven-day candles in glass

jars that can be found in metaphysical shops, botanicas, and even grocery stores in areas with high Latinx concentrations. The most popular saints and folk saints have jar candles with their image and prayer printed right on the jar. While these specialized candles used to be the sole domain of Catholic saints and folk saints, these days it's not difficult to find similarly styled candles with the images of beloved pop culture figures from Anthony Bourdain to Prince via a quick internet search. Of course, if a practitioner is creatively inclined, decorating a plain jar candle with art, quotations, or symbols of a pop culture folk saint is easily done and can add a fair amount of personalized energy to the candle. In Catholic practice these candles can be used with a one-time prayer; however, they are often used in the course of a *novena*, a nine-day devotional practice.

To perform a novena for a pop culture folk saint one would need to create either one prayer, petition, or devotional incantation to be repeated on nine successive days or create nine unique prayers. Each day the petitioner would light the candle, say the appropriate prayer, and then let the candle burn for a set amount of time—an hour is common. It is not unusual for the same candle to be used for multiple petitions or many novenas, as opposed to being burnt completely for each petition. If a practitioner is unable or does not wish to burn a candle, a similar effect can be made by placing an electric tea light in an appropriately decorated glass jar. The traditional practice of devotionally lighting candles is easily adapted for use with pop culture folk saints.

Make an Offering

Another traditional method of working with folk saints is to promise an offering in exchange for aid. The practice of making offerings in order to solicit aid should be familiar to any magickal practitioner who works with metaphysical entities of any kind. In magickal practice it's common to make physical offerings such as food, drink, flowers, candles, or incense to metaphysical entities, and all of these can also be offered to folk saints.

In Latin America folk saints are also commonly offered small metal charms called *milagros* that represent the aid being solicited. For example, if one were asking El Niño Fidencio for help in healing a broken leg, one could offer a milagro in the shape of a leg. Such charms make excellent offerings for pop culture folk saints as well.

Traditional offerings to saints can also be service oriented rather than physical. Saints are frequently promised devotional acts, such as repeated prayers or the abstention from luxuries in the saint's name, or volunteerism, such as the promise to repair something in a shrine or work in a soup kitchen for a time. One can offer the same to a pop culture folk saint, particularly if the service act is directly linked to the interests of the figure. For example, a service offering to Steve Irwin could be volunteering in an animal shelter for a day.

Offerings should be large enough to show some effort on the part of the petitioner but need not be extravagant, and they should be tailored to both the request being made and the personality of the recipient.

A LITTLE BIT OF MAGIC

A great resource for pop culture folk saint candles is Omakase Images. They have candles ready to go for a whole host of pop culture figures. Visit omakase-ltd.squarepace .com/candles.

Thoughtful offerings are always an excellent way to petition pop culture folk saints.

Connect through Pop Culture

While traditional methods of petitioning Catholic folk saints work with pop culture folk saints, they are far from the only options. Pop culture figures can, and should, be connected with through pop culture. Simply enjoying the media inhabited by the pop culture figure can be considered a devotional act. If one wanted to work with John Lennon, one could simply listen to his music and ask for his help, no candles or elaborately written prayers necessary. Of course, taking up a guitar and performing one of his songs would be even better. Taking a bit of time and effort to do something special to connect with a pop culture folk saint will always add power and solidify the intent of your working. If one wanted to work with Nikola Tesla, one could build a miniature Tesla coil while watching a Tesla documentary as a devotional act, and the finished coil could be an offering.

Depending on the interests of the practitioner and the dominion of the pop culture folk saint, a practitioner could create a meme, share something on social media, make an altar of action figures, create fan art or fan fiction, or wear branded clothing to connect with that folk saint. There is virtually no limit to the ways one can connect with a pop culture persona. A creative practitioner can use the media of the pop culture folk saint as a mechanism to connect with their energies and perform effective magick.

Modern pop culture is filled with megastars and public personalities that are so adored that they both connect with us on a deep personal level and are elevated into something larger than life. As magickal practitioners, we can tap into the power of these public personas and work with them as we do other metaphysical entities. With a bit of creativity and the greatest respect we can make magickal allies of our real-life heroes and work with them as pop culture folk saints.

Color Correspondences

Color magic uses various hues to influence energy. It can attract or repel, strengthen or weaken. It expresses thoughts and feelings that don't fit easily into words. People choose colors of clothes, jewelry, walls, and carpet to create desired effects. In magic, we use altar cloths, candles, gemstones, bowls, and other altar tools to channel this energy. Coloring pages help people relax.

Different cultures may use different correspondences. Western cultures associate white with life and black with death; Eastern cultures tend to reverse those. It comes from interpretations. Red is the color of blood, which can suggest vitality or danger, depending on how you look at it. So there is no "right" or "wrong" meaning. Use the color associations that resonate with you.

Maroon: Crone, drama, respect, sensuality

Crimson: Determination, righteous anger, survival

Scarlet: Action, female sexuality, vitality

Red: Fire, strength, danger

Orange: Creativity, addiction, opportunity

Gold: God, sun, justice

Topaz: Male sexuality, memory, fast effects

Yellow: Air, joy, charm

Lime Green: Growth, speed, end frustration

Green: Envy, money, health

Teal: Acceptance, abundance, happy home

Turquoise: Work-life balance, guilt, receiving

Blue: Water, truth, family

Indigo: Will, spirit, psychic

Purple: Wisdom, emotions, power

Lavender: Knowledge, intuition, divination

Violet: Calm, gratitude, tension

Coral: Mother, nurturing, emotional energy

Pink: Love, compassion, partnership

Fuchsia: Fight depression, self-direction, self-worth

Rose: Maiden, romance, friendship

Brown: Earth, stability, memory

Tan: Construction, food, past life

Black: Dark Moon, defense, grounding

Gray: Balance, loneliness, rest

Silver: Goddess, Moon, dreams

White: Crescent Moon, purity, peace

Ivory: Full Moon, luxury, animal magic

Magical Coloring

Coloring, or any creative undertaking, allows us to express our true spirit and reminds us that we get to decide how to manifest our world. We choose our own vibe, we decide on colors, blends, methods of shading; once we make our mark, it becomes our own. In coloring, life, and magic, never be afraid to color outside the lines.

Carefully cut out the page on the right and incorporate it in a special blessing written for 2020!

Altar Blessing

This spell works nicely on the Full Moon. Light a white candle and your favorite incense, play some soothing music, and ground and center yourself.

Visualize yourself standing before the altar in this illustration. Add color to each tool while focusing on your own pure magic as they come to life! As you color the altar cloth, imagine how it feels as you smooth it over the altar. Would you light a candle next? Color the holders, candles, and finally the flames, activating their power. Is the chalice holding water, wine, or mead? Imagine the taste as you color the chalice. As you color each one, hear the tone of the bell and feel the wand and athame in your hand. The cat rests his front paws on the pentacle, a reservoir for magical power; bring them both to life under your creative hand.

When you're finished, clean and reset your own altar, then set your artwork full of energy on it, allowing the magic you put into it to radiate out over your sacred space. If you're happy with how it turned out, you can put it in a small frame and hang it near your altar or use it as part of a travel altar kit.

—Mickie Mueller

The Phoenix

Our 2020 mascot is the phoenix, bringing us energies of rebirth and renewal. We've included a coloring page that may be cut out and included in a spell to use your challenges of the past as fuel to spark your renewal.

Legend of the Phoenix

The phoenix is a spirit creature, a bird of transformation and regeneration revered across many cultures, including those of Greece, Egypt, Phoenicia, and China. According to legend, as the phoenix becomes very old, it bursts into flames and is reborn from the ashes of its former self. In Greek stories it lives for five hundred years and dines on frankincense. According to Chinese tradition, the sighting of the phoenix foretells a new era of leadership bringing virtues of goodness, wisdom, kindness, duty, and reliability.

There are many descriptions of the hues of the phoenix, ranging from golden and fiery red shades to cool peacock blues, purples, and greens, so the colors that you choose are completely up to you.

Phoenix Correspondences
Elements: Fire, air
Sun Sign: Aquarius
Celestial Bodies: Sun, Mars
Magical Properties: Rebirth, renewal, resilience, healing, strength, protection
Deities: Osiris, Apollo, Ra,
Herbs: Frankincense, myrrh, palm, willow, cinnamon, cardamom

Phoenix Spell for Renewal

Time this spell for a New Moon.

You will need:
Phoenix illustration
Coloring medium of your choice
1 white seven-day candle
Several sticks of frankincense incense or incense of your choice

As you color the flames at the bottom of this art focus on the things that you wish to release from your life. These things will be banished through flame becoming fuel for your renewal. Once the flames are complete, leave them behind and move on to the phoenix itself. Shift your focus upon your goals now. Visualize yourself renewed as you color. Once the magical art you've created is complete, using a glue stick, attach it to the front of a white seven-day candle.

As you light the candle, use this charm to activate it:

I now release the dark and blight,
Casting it to kindling now alight.
My spirit rises from the flame.
Renewed, I rise and stake my claim.

Light the candle and let it burn. Extinguish the flame when you can't attend it, and relight it again using an incense stick and repeating the charm. Light it every day for as long as it takes to burn out. When the candle is finally burned away, the spell is complete.

—*Mickie Mueller*

Contributors

ELIZABETH BARRETTE has been involved with the Pagan community for more than twenty-seven years. She has served as managing editor of PanGaia and dean of studies at the Grey School of Wizardry. Her book *Composing Magic: How to Create Magical Spells, Rituals, Blessings, Chants, and Prayers* explains how to combine writing and spirituality. She lives in central Illinois. Visit her blog *The Wordsmith's Forge* (ysabetwordsmith.livejournal.com) or website Pen-Ultimate Productions (penultimateproductions.weebly.com).

DANIELLE BLACKWOOD is the astrology columnist for *Sage-Woman* magazine and Banyen Books and Sound and has studied and practiced astrology for more than thirty years. As a priestess, she has been facilitating workshops, classes, ceremony, and retreats on astrology and women's mysteries since 1994. Visit Danielle online at danielleblackwood.com.

BLAKE OCTAVIAN BLAIR is a shamanic and druidic practitioner, ordained minister, writer, Usui Reiki Master-Teacher, and musical artist. Blake blends mystical traditions from both the East and West along with a reverence for the natural world into his own brand of spirituality. He is an avid reader, knitter, and pescatarian. Blake lives in New England with his beloved husband. Visit him on the web at blakeoctavianblair.com or write to him at blake@blake octavianblair.com.

EMILY CARLIN is a Witch, writer, teacher, mediator, and ritual presenter based in Seattle, Washington. She currently teaches one-on-one online and at in-person events on the West Coast. For more information and links to her blogs, go to about.me/ecarlin.

DEBORAH CASTELLANO (Bridgewater, New Jersey) is a writer, crafter, and glamour girl who serves as a frequent contributor to occult and Pagan sources such as *Witchvox*, *PaganSquare*, and *Witches & Pagans*.

KERRI CONNOR is the author of *The Pocket Spell Creator*, *The Pocket Guide to Rituals*, *The Pocket Idiot's Guide to Potions*, and *Spells for Tough Times*. High Priestess of the Gathering Grove, she has been published in several magazines and is a frequent contributor to Llewellyn's almanacs. A graduate from the University of Wisconsin, Kerri holds a BA in communications and lives with her family, cats, and chickens in rural Illinois.

DIVINA CORNICK is a writer, yoga instructor, and Gray Witch living in South Carolina with her dog. She holds a BA in international studies and loves to skydive, read, hike, and garden. She specializes in weaving magic on the yoga mat, bringing movement to the Craft and using the body to focus the mind and ignite the soul. You can follow her adventures on divinacornick.blogspot.com, instagram.com/divinacornick, and instagram.com/yogascopes.

MONICA CROSSON is the author of *The Magickal Family: Pagan Living in Harmony with Nature* and *Summer Sage*. She is a Master Gardener who lives in the beautiful Pacific Northwest, happily digging in the dirt and tending her raspberries with her family and their small menagerie of farm animals. She has been a practicing Witch for thirty years and is a member of Evergreen Coven. Monica is a regular contributor to Llewellyn's annuals as well as *Enchanted Living* magazine and *Witchology* magazine.

RAVEN DIGITALIS (Missoula, Montana) is the author of *The Everyday Empath, Esoteric Empathy, Shadow Magick Compendium, Plan-*

etary Spells & Rituals, and *Goth Craft.* He is the cofounder of a non-profit multicultural temple called Opus Aima Obscuræ (OAO), which primarily observes Neopagan and Hindu traditions. Raven has been an earth-based practitioner since 1999, a Priest since 2003, a Freemason since 2012, and an empath all his life. Visit him at ravendigitalis.com and www.opusaimaobscurae.org.

KATE FREULER lives in Ontario, Canada, with her husband and daughter. She owns and operates whitemoonwitchcraft.com, an online Witchcraft boutique. When she isn't crafting spells and amulets for clients or herself, she loves to write, paint, read, draw, and create.

SASHA GRAHAM is the author of *Tarot Diva, 365 Tarot Spreads, 365 Tarot Spells,* and *Llewellyn's Complete Book of the Rider-Waite-Smith Tarot.* She is the editor of and contributor to *Tarot Fundamentals, Tarot Experience,* and *Tarot Compendium.* Her tarot decks include the Haunted House Tarot and Dark Wood Tarot. Sasha hosts *The Enchanted Kitchen,* a short-form magical cooking series for YouTube and Heyou Media's *Mobile. Mini. Movies.*

JD HORTWORT resides in North Carolina. She is an avid student of herbology and gardening. She has written a weekly garden column since 1991. She is a professional, award-winning author, journalist and magazine editor, as well as a frequent contributor to the Llewellyn annuals. Recently retired from journalism, she continues to write on topics as diverse as gardening and NASCAR. When not at the keyboard, she spends time in her own landscape, taking trips with friends wherever the road leads and with her nose buried in a book.

JAMES KAMBOS became interested in magic and folklore by watching his Greek grandmother perform folk magic rituals. Today he writes many articles about magic, herbs, and folklore. He graduated from Ohio University. He lives in the beautiful hill country of southern Ohio.

LUPA is a naturalist Pagan author and artist in the Pacific Northwest. She is the author of several books on nature-based Paganism, including *Nature Spirituality From the Ground Up: Connect With Totems In Your Ecosystem* (Llewellyn, 2016). She is also the creator of the Tarot of Bones deck and book. You can find out more about Lupa and her works at thegreenwolf.com.

ESTHA K. V. MCNEVIN is a priestess and Eastern Hellenistic oracle of Opus Aima Obscuræ. Since 2003, she has dedicated her time as a ceremonialist psychic, lecturer, freelance author, and artist. Among hosting public sabbats, Estha organizes annual philanthropic fundraisers, teaches classes, manages the temple farm, leads Full Moon spellcrafting ceremonies, and officiates for the women's divination rituals each Dark Moon. To learn more, please explore opusaimaobscurae.org and facebook.com/opusaimaobscurae.

DANIEL MOLER is a writer, artist, educator, and shamanic practitioner. He has published fiction and nonfiction works around the world in magazines, in journals, in gaming modules, and online, including *Positive Health Magazine, Cannabis Culture, The Tattooed Buddha, Sacred Hoop, Elephant Journal,* and *A Journal of Contemporary Shamanism.* He is the author of *Shamanic Qabalah, RED Mass,* and *Machine Elves 101.* Visit Daniel online at danielmolerweb.com.

THORN MOONEY is a Gardnerian priestess operating in Charlotte, North Carolina. She holds a graduate degree in religious studies, practices Historical European Martial Arts (HEMA), and works as a public high school teacher. Visit her online at thornthewitch.com.

MICKIE MUELLER explores magic and spirituality through art and the written word at her home studio and workshop in Missouri. She is the author and illustrator of *The Voice of the Trees,* the illustrator of *Mystical Cats Tarot* and *Magical Dogs Tarot,* and the author of *The Witch's Mirror* and *Llewellyn's Little Book of Halloween.* Since 2007, Mickie has been a regular article and illustration contributor to Llewellyn's annuals and many Llewellyn books.

DIANA RAJCHEL has written book reviews, articles, and books on Witchcraft for far longer than she cares to admit. She has a passion for dance, herbalism, tarot, and obscure folklore that she happily turns into spells. She serves as the city priestess of San Francisco, where she runs the Emperor Norton Pagan meetup. She also enjoys good burritos and a good hard laugh.

SILVER RAVENWOLF is perhaps best known as one of the most widely published Wiccan/Pagan authors of her time, including bestsellers *Solitary Witch, Teen Witch,* and *To Ride a Silver Broomstick.* Artist, doll maker, chandler, photographer, and internet entrepreneur, she also heads the Black Forest Clan Circle and Seminary, a Wiccan organization that consists of over sixty non-hiving covens. Wife of thirty-five years, mother of four grown children, and grandmother, Silver has been interviewed by the *New York Times,* the *Wall Street Journal,* the *US News & World Report,* and A&E's *Biography.* You can find Silver on Twitter, Instagram, Facebook, and WordPress (silverravenwolf.wordpress.com) or visit her at silverravenwolf.info.

MELISSA TIPTON is a licensed massage therapist, Reiki Master, and tarot reader who helps people live more magically through her healing practice, Life Alchemy Massage Therapy. She's the author of *Living Reiki: Heal Yourself and Transform Your Life,* and you can read more of her witchy writing, take online classes, and book tarot readings at getmomassage.com and yogiwitch.com. She loves digging in the garden, getting lost in a pile of books, and hiking with her husband in the woods (aka, looking for faeries).

CHARLYNN WALLS is a member of a local coven. She has been an active member in the local community working with organizations such as St. Louis Pagan Picnic and Witch School. She has been a practitioner of the Craft for over twenty years and currently resides in Central Missouri with her family. She continues to share her knowledge by teaching at local festivals and continuing to produce articles for Llewellyn Publications.

TESS WHITEHURST teaches magical and intuitive arts in live workshops and via her online community and learning hub, the Good Vibe Tribe Online School of Magical Arts. An award-winning author, she's written eight books, which have been translated into eighteen languages. She's appeared on Bravo, Fox, and NBC, and her writing has been featured in *Writer's Digest, Spirit and Destiny* (in the UK), and on her popular website, tesswhitehurst.com.

CHARLIE RAINBOW WOLF is happiest when she is creating something, especially if it can be made from items that others have cast aside. Pottery, writing, knitting, astrology, and tarot are her deepest interests, but she happily confesses that she's easily distracted because life offers so many wonderful things to explore. A recorded singer-songwriter and a published author, she is an advocate of organic gardening and cooking and lives in the Midwest with her husband and special-needs Great Danes. Visit www.charlie rainbow.com.